MW00737271

BLUEPRINTS: A PROBLEM NOTEBOOK
FUNDAMENTALS OF FINANCIAL MANAGEMENT:
THE CONCISE EDITION

EUGENE F. BRIGHAM
AND
JOEL F. HOUSTON
UNIVERSITY OF FLORIDA

The Dryden Press
Harcourt Brace College Publishers

Fort Worth   Philadelphia   San Diego   New York   Orlando   Austin   San Antonio
Toronto   Montreal   London   Sydney   Tokyo

Cover image: Lamberto Alvarez

Copyright © 1996 by Harcourt Brace & Company

All rights reserved. No part of this publication may be reproduced or transmitted in any form or by any means, electronic or mechanical, including photocopy, recording, or any information storage and retrieval system, without permission in writing from the publisher.

Although for mechanical reasons all pages of this publication are perforated, only those pages imprinted with Harcourt Brace & Company are intended for removal.

Requests for permission to make copies of any part of the work should be mailed to: Permissions Department, Harcourt Brace & Company, 6277 Sea Harbor Drive, Orlando, Florida 32887-6777.

Address for Editorial Correspondence
The Dryden Press, 301 Commerce Street, Suite 3700, Fort Worth, TX 76102

Address for Orders
The Dryden Press, 6277 Sea Harbor Drive, Orlando, FL 32887
1-800-782-4479, or 1-800-433-0001 (in Florida)

ISBN: 0-03-015973-3

Printed in the United States of America

5 6 7 8 9 0 1 2 3 4   095   9 8 7 6 5 4 3 2 1

The Dryden Press
Harcourt Brace College Publishers

Blueprints has become an integral part of the material we provide to students. At the University of Florida, we teach a large class, with upwards of 500 students each semester. This large class size forces us to lecture, even though we prefer discussion oriented classes. To get the students more involved, we have developed a set of integrated cases which cover the key points in each chapter and which we use as the basis for our lectures. For our classes, we use the computer slideshow to present the material that is summarized in each integrated case. Early on, students began asking us to make copies of the slides available to them. We did so, and that improved the class considerably. With paper copies of the slides, students could focus on what was being said in the lecture without having to copy things down for later review. *Blueprints* includes a copy of each integrated case, copies of the slides, and space to write down additional notes.

We consider the current version quite complete. However, the <u>optimal</u> product varies from instructor to instructor, depending on how the class is conducted. Therefore, instructors are encouraged to modify *Blueprints* to suit their own styles and interests. For example, if one covers chapters in a different order, or does not cover certain chapters, or covers only part of some chapters, or has additional materials not covered in the text, or anything else, the *Blueprints* chapters can be rearranged, added to or subtracted from, or modified in any other way. Deletions and rearrangements are easy, but additions and/or modifications would, of course, require some typing and/or cutting and pasting.

Students always want copies of old exams. Also, we have review sessions, conducted by TAs, and those sessions are devoted to working exam-type problems. So, we have included a number of exam-type problems at the end of each *Blueprints* chapter. Students work them on their own or else go to review sessions where the TAs work them. The solutions for these exam-type problems are provided at the end of the last *Blueprints* chapter.

Currently, at Florida we provide an off-campus copy shop with the *Blueprints* chapter material. Of course, we provide materials only for those chapters which we plan to cover in the course.

Instructors can use *Blueprints* in conjunction with the computer slideshow, which is based on the integrated cases. Also, we frequently use the blackboard, both to explain the calculations which lie behind some of the numbers and to provide different examples. Our students end up with lots of marginal notes which clarify various points.

One thing has become crystal clear over the years--the best lecture notes, and materials related thereto, are instructor-specific. It is difficult to use someone else's notes verbatim. However, there is no point in reinventing the wheel, and if the *Blueprints* wheel fits a particular instructor's wagon, he or she might do well to use it, spending time adapting it to his or her own style and coverage rather than taking the time to develop lectures notes de novo. Therefore, you are encouraged to look over the *Blueprints* package, decide if and how you might use it, and then go to it. If you are like us, you will change things from semester to semester--there is no such thing as static optimality!

If you do use the package, and find some modifications that work well for you, we would very much appreciate hearing from you--your modifications might well help us and others.

Eugene F. Brigham
Joel F. Houston

P.O. Box 117160
College of Business
University of Florida
Gainesville, Florida 32611-7160

June 1995

SUGGESTIONS FOR STUDENTS USING BLUEPRINTS

1. Read the textbook chapter first, going through the entire chapter rapidly. Don't expect to understand everything on this first reading, but do try to get a good idea of what the chapter covers, the key terms, and the like. <u>It is useful to read the chapter before the first lecture on it.</u>

2. You could also read the *Blueprints* chapter material before class, but that is not necessary.

3. *Blueprints* was designed as the basis for a lecture--the most important material in each chapter is covered, and the material most likely to give you trouble is emphasized. As your instructor goes through *Blueprints*, you should (1) see what we regard as the most important material and (2) get a better feel for how to think about issues and work relevant problems.

4. You could read *Blueprints*, in connection with the text, and get a reasonably good idea of what is going on in the course. However, the real value of *Blueprints* is as a vehicle to help the class lecture make more sense and to help you get a good set of notes. In class, your instructor will discuss various points raised in *Blueprints* and elaborate on different issues. Also, he or she will explain how formulas are used, where data in tables come from, and the like. <u>You will end up with lots of marginal notes on your copy if you use *Blueprints* as it is supposed to be used.</u> Indeed, these marginal notes will constitute your class notes.

BLUEPRINTS
Table of Contents

BLUEPRINTS: CHAPTER 1
AN OVERVIEW OF FINANCIAL MANAGEMENT

There is no integrated case for Chapter 1. Begin with slides.

Copyright © 1996 by The Dryden Press. All rights reserved.

CHAPTER 1
An Overview of Financial Management

Career Opportunities in Finance:

- Money and capital markets
- Investments
- Financial management

Financial Management Issues of the 1990s:

- Use of computers and electronic transfers of information
- The globalization of business

Copyright © 1996 by The Dryden Press. All rights reserved.

Responsibilities of the Financial Staff:

- **Forecasting and planning**
- **Investment and financing decisions**
- **Coordination and control**
- **Transactions in the financial markets**

Alternative Forms of Business Organization:

- **Sole proprietorship**
- **Partnership**
- **Corporation**

Sole Proprietorship:

- **Advantages:**
  - **Ease of formation**
  - **Subject to few regulations**
  - **No corporate income taxes**
- **Disadvantages:**
  - **Limited life**
  - **Unlimited liability**
  - **Difficult to raise capital**

BLUEPRINTS: CHAPTER 1

Copyright © 1996 by The Dryden Press. All rights reserved.

Partnership:

- A partnership has roughly the same advantages and disadvantages as a sole proprietorship.

Corporation:

- Advantages:
  - Unlimited life
  - Easy transfer of ownership
  - Limited liability
  - Ease of raising capital
- Disadvantages:
  - Double taxation
  - Cost of set-up and report filing

Goals of the Corporation:

- The primary goal is shareholder wealth maximization, which translates to maximizing stock price.
  - Do firms have any responsibilities to society at large?
  - Is stock price maximization good or bad for society?
  - Should firms behave ethically?

Copyright © 1996 by The Dryden Press. All rights reserved.

Agency Relationships:

- An agency relationship exists whenever a principal hires an agent to act on their behalf.
- Within a corporation, agency relationships exist between
    - Shareholders and managers
    - Shareholders and creditors

Shareholders versus Managers:

- Managers are naturally inclined to act in their own best interests.
- But the following factors affect managerial behavior:
    - The threat of firing
    - The threat of takeover
    - Managerial compensation plans

Shareholders versus Creditors:

- Shareholders (through managers) could take actions to maximize stock price that are detrimental to creditors.
- In the long run, such actions will raise the cost of debt and ultimately lower stock price.

Copyright © 1996 by The Dryden Press. All rights reserved.

Factors Influenced by Managers that Affect Stock Price:

- **Projected earnings per share**
- **Timing of the earnings stream**
- **Riskiness of the earnings stream**
- **Use of debt (capital structure)**
- **Dividend policy**

BLUEPRINTS: CHAPTER 1

Copyright © 1996 by The Dryden Press. All rights reserved.

EXAM-TYPE PROBLEMS

1. Which of the following statements is most correct?

   a. Proxy fights and hostile takeovers are the two main methods of transferring ownership interest in a corporation.

   b. The corporation is a legal entity created by the state and is a direct extension of the legal status of its owners and managers, that is, the owners and managers <u>are</u> the corporation.

   c. Unlimited liability and limited life are two key advantages of the corporate form over other forms of business organization.

   d. Due in large part to limited liability and ease of ownership transfer, corporations have less trouble raising money in financial markets than other organizational forms.

   e. The stockholders of the corporation are insulated by limited legal liability, and the legal status of the corporation protects the firm's managers from civil and criminal charges arising from business operations.

2. Which of the following statements is most correct?

   a. The proper goal of the financial manager should be to maximize the firm's expected cash flow, because this will add the most wealth to each of the individual shareholders (owners) of the firm.

   b. One way to state the decision framework most useful for carrying out the firm's objective is as follows: "The financial manager should seek that combination of assets, liabilities, and capital which will generate the largest expected projected after-tax income over the relevant time horizon."

   c. The riskiness inherent in a firm's earnings per share (EPS) depends on the characteristics of the projects the firm selects, which means it depends upon the firm's assets, but EPS does not depend on the manner in which those assets are financed.

   d. Since large, publicly-owned firms are controlled by their management teams, and typically, ownership is widely dispersed, managers have great freedom in managing the firm. Managers may operate in the stockholders' best interest, but they may also operate in their own personal best interests. As long as managers stay within the law, there simply aren't any effective controls over managerial decisions in such situations.

   e. Agency problems exist between stockholders and managers, and between stockholders and creditors.

Copyright © 1996 by The Dryden Press. All rights reserved.

2-11 Donna Jamison, a 1993 graduate of the University of Florida with two years of banking experience, was recently brought in as assistant to the chairman of the board of D'Leon Inc., a small food producer which operates in north Florida and whose specialty is high-quality pecan and other nut products sold in the snack-foods market. D'Leon's president, Al Watkins, decided in 1994 to undertake a major expansion and to "go national" in competition with Frito-Lay, Eagle, and other major snack food companies. Watkins felt that D'Leon's products were of a higher quality than the competition's, that this quality differential would enable it to charge a premium price, and that the end result would be greatly increased sales, profits, and stock price.

The company doubled its plant capacity, opened new sales offices outside its home territory, and launched an expensive advertising campaign. D'Leon's results were not satisfactory, to put it mildly. Its board of directors, which consisted of its president and vice-president plus its major stockholders (who were all local business people) was most upset when directors learned how the expansion was going. Suppliers were being paid late and were unhappy, and the bank was complaining about the deteriorating situation and threatening to cut off credit. As a result, President Watkins was informed that changes would have to be made, and quickly, or he would be fired. Also, at the board's insistence Donna Jamison was brought in and given the job of assistant to Fred Campo, a retired banker who was D'Leon's chairman and largest stockholder. Campo agreed to give up a few of his golfing days and to help nurse the company back to health, with Jamison's help.

Jamison began by gathering the financial statements and other data given in Tables IC2-1, IC2-2, and IC2-3. Assume that you are Jamison's assistant, and you must help her answer the following questions for Campo. (Note: We will continue with this case in Chapter 3, and you will feel more comfortable with the analysis there, but answering these questions will help prepare you for Chapter 3. Provide clear explanations, not yes or no answers!)

Copyright © 1996 by The Dryden Press. All rights reserved.

Table IC2-1. Balance Sheets

	1995	1994
Assets:		
Cash	$ 7,282	$ 57,600
Accounts receivable	632,160	351,200
Inventories	1,287,360	715,200
Total current assets	$1,926,802	$1,124,000
Gross fixed assets	$1,202,950	$ 491,000
Less accumulated depreciation	263,160	146,200
Net fixed assets	$ 939,790	$ 344,800
Total assets	$2,866,592	$1,468,800
Liabilities and equity:		
Accounts payable	$ 524,160	$ 145,600
Notes payable	720,000	200,000
Accruals	489,600	136,000
Total current liabilities	$1,733,760	$ 481,600
Long-term debt	$1,000,000	$ 323,432
Common stock (100,000 shares)	$ 460,000	$ 460,000
Retained earnings	(327,168)	203,768
Total equity	$ 132,832	$ 663,768
Total liabilities and equity	$2,866,592	$1,468,800

Copyright © 1996 by The Dryden Press. All rights reserved.

Table IC2-2. Income Statements

	1995	1994
Sales	$5,834,400	$3,432,000
Cost of goods sold	5,728,000	2,864,000
Other expenses	680,000	340,000
Depreciation	116,960	18,900
Total operating costs	$6,524,960	$3,222,900
EBIT	($ 690,560)	$ 209,100
Interest expense	176,000	62,500
EBT	($ 866,560)	$ 146,600
Taxes (40%)	(346,624)	58,640
Net income	($ 519,936)	$ 87,960
EPS	($5.199)	$0.880
DPS	$0.110	$0.220
Book value per share	$1.328	$6.638
Stock price	$2.250	$8.500
Shares outstanding	100,000	100,000
Tax rate	40.00%	40.00%
Lease payments	40,000	40,000
Sinking fund payments	0	0

Copyright © 1996 by The Dryden Press. All rights reserved.

Table IC2-3. Statement of Cash Flows, 1995

Operating activities:
    Net income   ($ 519,936)

Additions (sources of cash):
    Depreciation   116,960
    Increase in accounts payable   378,560
    Increase in accruals   353,600

Subtractions (uses of cash):
    Increase in accounts receivable   (280,960)
    Increase in inventories   (572,160)
Net cash provided by oper. activities   ($ 523,936)

Long-term investing activities:
    Cash used to acquire fixed assets   ($ 711,950)

Financing activities:
    Increase in notes payable $ 520,000
    Increase in long-term debt   676,568
    Payment of cash dividends   (11,000)
Net cash provided by financing activities $1,185,568

Sum: Net decrease in cash   ($ 50,318)
Plus: Cash at beginning of year   57,600

Cash at end of year $ 7,282

Copyright © 1996 by The Dryden Press. All rights reserved.

a. Refer to Figure 2-1 in Chapter 2. What happened to D'Leon's "cash reservoir" rectangle during 1995? What happened to the other asset and liability reservoirs?

b. D'Leon purchases materials on 30-day terms, meaning that it is supposed to pay for purchases within 30 days of receipt. Judging from its 1995 balance sheet, do you think D'Leon pays suppliers on time? Explain. If not, what problems might this lead to?

c. D'Leon spends money for labor, materials, and fixed assets (depreciation) to make products, and still more money to sell those products. Then, it makes sales which result in receivables, which eventually result in cash inflows. Does it appear that D'Leon's sales price exceeds its costs per unit sold? How does this affect the "cash reservoir," or cash balance?

d. Suppose D'Leon's sales manager told the sales staff to start offering 60-day credit terms rather than the 30-day terms now being offered. D'Leon's competitors react by offering similar terms, so sales remain constant. What effect would this have on the cash account? How would the cash account be affected if sales doubled as a result of the credit policy change?

e. Can you imagine a situation in which the sales price exceeds the cost of producing and selling a unit of output, yet a dramatic increase in sales volume causes the cash balance to decline?

f. In general, could a company like D'Leon increase sales without a corresponding increase in inventory and other assets? Would the asset increase occur before the increase in sales, and, if so, how would that affect the cash account and the statement of cash flows?

g. Did D'Leon finance its expansion program with internally generated funds (additions to retained earnings plus depreciation) or with external capital? How does the choice of financing affect the company's financial strength?

h. Refer to Tables IC2-2 and IC2-3. Suppose D'Leon broke even in 1995 in the sense that sales revenues equaled total operating costs plus interest charges. Would the asset expansion have caused the company to experience a cash shortage which required it to raise external capital?

i. If D'Leon started depreciating fixed assets over 7 years rather than 10 years, would that affect (1) the physical stock of assets, (2) the balance sheet account for fixed assets, (3) the company's reported net income, and (4) its cash position? Assume the

Copyright © 1996 by The Dryden Press. All rights reserved.

same depreciation method is used for stockholder reporting and for tax calculations, and the accounting change has no effect on assets' physical lives.

j. Explain how (1) inventory valuation methods, (2) the accounting policy regarding expensing versus capitalizing research and development, and (3) the policy with regard to funding future retirement plan costs (retirement pay and retirees' health benefits) could affect the financial statements.

k. D'Leon's stock sells for $2.25 per share even though the company had large losses. Does the positive stock price indicate that some investors are irrational?

l. D'Leon followed the standard practice of paying dividends on a quarterly basis. It paid a dividend during the first two quarters of 1995, then eliminated the dividend when management realized that a loss would be incurred for the year. The dividend was cut before the losses were announced, and at that point the stock price fell from $8.50 to $3.50. Why would an $0.11, or even a $0.22, dividend reduction lead to a $5.00 stock price reduction?

m. Explain how earnings per share, dividends per share, and book value per share are calculated, and what they mean. Why does the market price per share *not* equal the book value per share?

n. How much new money did D'Leon borrow from its bank during 1995? How much additional credit did its suppliers extend? Its employees and the taxing authorities?

o. If you were D'Leon's banker, or the credit manager of one of its suppliers, would you be worried about your job? If you were a current D'Leon employee, a retiree, or a stockholder, should you be concerned?

p. The 1995 income statement shows negative taxes, that is, a tax credit. How much taxes would the company have had to pay in the past to actually get this credit? If taxes paid within the last 3 years had been less than $346,624, what would have happened? Would this have affected the statement of cash flows and the ending cash balance?

q. Working with Jamison has required you to put in a lot of overtime, so you have had very little time to spend on your private finances. It's now April 1, and you have only two weeks left to file your income tax return. You have managed to get all the information together that you will need to complete your return. D'Leon paid you a salary of $45,000, and you received $3,000 in dividends from common stock that you

Copyright © 1996 by The Dryden Press. All rights reserved.

own. You are single, so your personal exemption is $2,450, and your itemized deductions are $4,550.

  (1)　On the basis of the information above and the 1994 individual tax rate schedule, what is your tax liability?

  (2)　What are your marginal and average tax rates?

r.　Assume that a corporation has $100,000 of taxable income from operations plus $5,000 of interest income and $10,000 of dividend income. What is the company's tax liability?

s.　Assume that after paying your personal income tax as calculated in Part q, you have $5,000 to invest. You have narrowed your investment choices down to California bonds with a yield of 7 percent or equally risky Exxon bonds with a yield of 10 percent. Which one should you choose and why? At what marginal tax rate would you be indifferent to the choice between California and Exxon bonds?

Copyright © 1996 by The Dryden Press. All rights reserved.

CHAPTER 2
Financial Statements, Cash Flow, and Taxes

- Balance Sheet
- Income Statement
- Statement of Cash Flows
- Cash Flow Cycle within Firm
- Personal Taxes
- Corporate Taxes

Balance Sheet: Assets

	1995	1994
Cash	7,282	57,600
AR	632,160	351,200
Inventories	1,287,360	715,200
Total CA	1,926,802	1,124,000
Gross FA	1,202,950	491,000
Less: Deprec.	263,160	146,200
Net FA	939,790	344,800
Total assets	2,866,592	1,468,800

Liab. & Equity

	1995	1994
Accounts payable	524,160	145,600
Notes payable	720,000	200,000
Accruals	489,600	136,000
Total CL	1,733,760	481,600
Long-term debt	1,000,000	323,432
Common stock	460,000	460,000
Retained earnings	(327,168)	203,768
Total equity	132,832	663,768
Total L & E	2,866,592	1,468,800

Copyright © 1996 by The Dryden Press. All rights reserved.

Income Statement

	1995	1994
Sales	5,834,400	3,432,000
COGS	5,728,000	2,864,000
Other expenses	680,000	340,000
Deprn.	116,960	18,900
Tot. op. costs	6,524,960	3,222,900
EBIT	(690,560)	209,100
Interest exp.	176,000	62,500
EBT	(866,560)	146,600
Taxes (40%)	(346,624)	58,640
Net income	(519,936)	87,960

Other Data

	1995	1994
No. of shares	100,000	100,000
EPS	($5.199)	$0.88
DPS	$0.110	$0.22
Stock price	$2.25	$8.50
Lease pmts	$40,000	$40,000

Statement of CFs (1995)

OPERATING ACTIVITIES	
Net income	(519,936)
Add (sources of cash):	
Depreciation	116,960
Increase in A/P	378,560
Increase in accruals	353,600
Subtract (uses of cash):	
Increase in A/R	(280,960)
Increase in inventories	(572,160)
Net cash provided by ops.	(523,936)

Copyright © 1996 by The Dryden Press. All rights reserved.

L-T INVESTING ACTIVITIES
Investment in fixed assets   (711,950)

FINANCING ACTIVITIES
Increase in notes payable   520,000
Increase in long-term debt   676,568
Payment of cash dividends   (11,000)
Net cash from financing   1,185,568

NET CHANGE IN CASH   (50,318)

Plus: Cash at beg. of year   57,600
Cash at end of year   7,282

What can you conclude about D'Leon's financial condition from its statement of CFs?

- Net CF from operations = -$523,936, mainly because of negative NI.
- The firm borrowed $1,185,568 to meets its cash requirements.
- Even after borrowing, the cash account fell by $50,318.

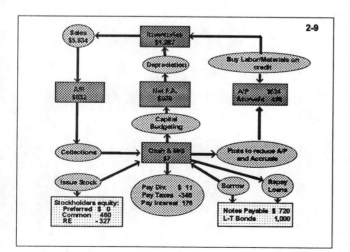

Copyright © 1996 by The Dryden Press. All rights reserved.

Does D'Leon pay its suppliers on time?

- Probably not.
- A/P increased 260% over the past year, while sales increased by only 70%.
- If this continues, suppliers may cut off D'Leon's trade credit.

Does it appear that D'Leon's sales price exceeds its cost per unit sold?

- No, the decline in the company's cash position suggests that D'Leon is spending more cash than it is taking in.

What effect would each of these actions have on D'Leon's cash account?

1. The company offers 60-day credit terms. The improved terms are matched by its competitors, so sales remain constant.
   - A/R would ↑
   - Cash would ↓

Copyright © 1996 by The Dryden Press. All rights reserved.

2. Sales double as a result of the change in credit terms.

- **Short-run: Inventory and Fixed Assets↑ to meet increased sales. A/R↑, Cash↓. Company may have to seek additional financing.**
- **Long-run: Collections increase and the company's cash position would improve.**

How did D'Leon finance its expansion?

- **D'Leon financed its expansion with external capital.**
- **D'Leon issued long-term debt which reduced its financial strength.**

Would D'Leon have required external capital if they had broken even in 1995?

- **Yes, the company would still have to finance its increase in assets.**

Copyright © 1996 by The Dryden Press. All rights reserved.

What happens if D'Leon depreciates its fixed assets over 7 years (as opposed to the current 10 years)?

- No effect on physical assets.
- Fixed assets on balance sheet would decline.
- Net income would decline.
- Tax payments would decline.
- Cash position would improve.

Other policies which can affect financial statements:

- Inventory valuation methods.
- Capitalization of R & D expenses.
- Policies for funding the company's retirement plan.

Does the company's positive stock price ($2.25), in the face of large losses, suggest that investors are irrational?

- No, it means that investors expect things to get better in the future.

Copyright © 1996 by The Dryden Press. All rights reserved.

Why did the stock fall after the dividend was cut?

- Management was "signalling" that the firm's operations were in trouble.
- The dividend cut lowered expectations for future profits which caused the stock price to decline.

What were some other sources of financing to D'Leon in 1995?

- Bank loans: Notes payable increased by $520,000.
- Credit from suppliers: A/P increased by $378,560.
- Employees: Accruals increased by $353,600.

D'Leon received a tax credit of $346,624 in 1995.

- This suggests the company paid at least $346,624 in taxes during the past 3 years.
- If D'Leon's payments over the past 3 years were less than $346,624, the firm would have had to carry forward the amount of its loss that was not carried back.
- If the firm did not receive a full refund, its cash position would be even worse.

BLUEPRINTS: CHAPTER 2

Copyright © 1996 by The Dryden Press. All rights reserved.

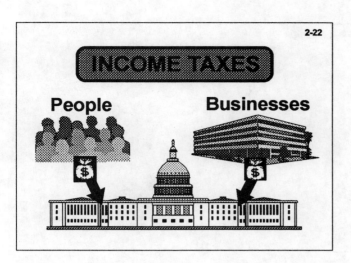

2-22

INCOME TAXES

People

Businesses

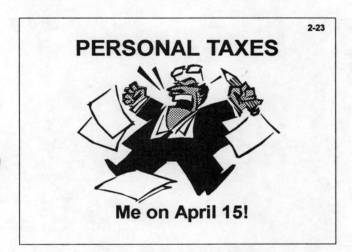

2-23

PERSONAL TAXES

Me on April 15!

2-24

1994 Single Individual Tax Rates:

Taxable Income	Tax on Base	Rate*
0 - 22,750	0	15%
22,750 - 55,100	3,413	28%
55,100 - 115,000	12,471	31%
115,000 - 250,000	31,040	36%
Over 250,000	79,640	39.6%

*Plus this percentage on the
the amount over the bracket base.

Copyright © 1996 by The Dryden Press. All rights reserved.

Assume your salary is $45,000, and you received $3,000 in dividends. You are single, so your personal exemption is $2,450 and your itemized deductions are $4,550.

On the basis of the info. above and the 1994 tax rate schedule, what is your tax liability?

Calculation of Taxable Income:

Salary	$45,000
Dividends	3,000
Personal exemptions	(2,450)
Deductions	(4,550)
Taxable Income	**$41,000**

- **Tax Liability:**   41,000 - 22,750

$$TL = \$3,413 + 0.28(\$18,250)$$
$$= \$8,523 .$$

- **Marginal Tax Rate = 28% .**

- **Average Tax Rate:**

$$\text{Tax rate} = \frac{8,523}{41,000} = 20.79\% .$$

BLUEPRINTS: CHAPTER 2
Copyright © 1996 by The Dryden Press. All rights reserved.

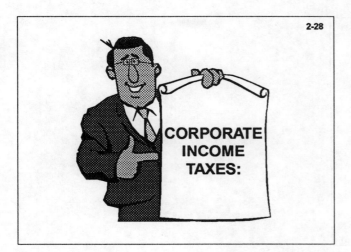

CORPORATE
INCOME
TAXES:

2-28

1994 Corporate Tax Rates:

2-29

Taxable Income	Tax on Base	Rate*
0 - 50,000	0	15%
50,000 - 75,000	7,500	25%
75,000 - 100,000	13,750	34%
100,000 - 335,000	22,250	39%
:	:	:
Over 18.3M	6.4M	35%

*Plus this percentage on the amount over the bracket base.

2-30

Assume a corporation has $100,000 of taxable income from operations, $5,000 of interest income, and $10,000 of dividend income.

What's its tax liability?

Copyright © 1996 by The Dryden Press. All rights reserved.

Operating income	$100,000
Interest income	5,000
Taxable dividend income	3,000
Taxable income	$108,000*

Tax = $22,250 + 0.39($8,000)

= $25,370 .

*Dividends - Exclusion
= 10,000 - 0.7(10,000) = 3,000.

Taxable vs. Tax Exempt Bonds

State and local government bonds (munis) are generally exempt from federal taxes.

- Exxon bonds at 10% vs. California muni bonds at 7%.
- T = Tax rate = 28%.
- After-tax interest income:

Exxon = 0.10(5,000)

− 0.10(5,000)(0.28)

= 0.10(5,000)(0.72) = 360 .

CAL = 0.07(5,000) − 0 = 350 .

Copyright © 1996 by The Dryden Press. All rights reserved.

2-34

At what tax rate would you be indifferent to muni vs. corp?

Solve for T in this eqn:

Muni Yield = Corp Yield(1 - T)

$$7.00\% = 10.0\%(1 - T)$$

$$7.00\% = 10.0\% - 10.0\%(T)$$

$$10.0\%(T) = 3.0\%$$

$$T = 3.0\%/0.10$$

$$T = 30.0\%.$$

2-35

Implications:

- If T > 30%, buy tax exempt munis.

- If T < 30%, buy corporate bonds.

- Only high income people should buy munis.

Copyright © 1996 by The Dryden Press. All rights reserved.

EXAM-TYPE PROBLEMS

1. Which of the following statements is most correct?

   a. In order to avoid double taxation and to escape the frequently higher tax rate applied to capital gains, stockholders generally prefer to have corporations pay dividends rather than to retain their earnings and reinvest the money in the business. Thus, earnings should be retained only if the firm needs capital very badly and would have difficulty raising it from external sources.

   b. Under our current tax laws, when investors pay taxes on their dividend income, they are being subjected to a form of double taxation.

   c. The fact that a percentage of the interest received by one corporation, which is paid by another corporation, is excluded from taxable income has encouraged firms to use more debt financing relative to equity financing.

   d. If the tax laws stated that $0.50 out of every $1.00 of interest paid by a corporation was allowed as a tax-deductible expense, this would probably encourage companies to use more debt financing than they presently do, other things held constant.

   e. Statements b and d are both correct.

2. Solarcell Corporation has $20,000 which it plans to invest in marketable securities. It is choosing between AT&T bonds which yield 11%, State of Florida muni bonds which yield 8%, and AT&T preferred stock with a dividend yield of 9%. Solarcell's corporate tax rate is 40%, and 70% of the preferred stock dividends it receives are tax exempt. Assuming that the investments are equally risky and that Solarcell chooses strictly on the basis of after-tax returns, which security should be selected? Answer by giving the after-tax rate of return on the highest yielding security.

Copyright © 1996 by The Dryden Press. All rights reserved.

3-13 Part I of this case, presented in Chapter 2, discussed the situation that D'Leon Inc., a regional snack foods producer, was in after a 1995 expansion program. Like Borden Inc., D'Leon had increased plant capacity and undertaken a major marketing campaign in an attempt to "go national." Thus far, sales have not been up to the forecasted level, costs have been higher than were projected, and a large loss occurred in 1995 rather than the expected profit. As a result, its managers, directors, and investors are concerned about the firm's survival.

Donna Jamison was brought in as assistant to Fred Campo, D'Leon's chairman, who had the task of getting the company back into a sound financial position. D'Leon's 1994 and 1995 balance sheets and income statements, together with projections for 1996, are given in Tables IC3-1 and IC3-2. In addition, Table IC3-3 gives the company's 1994 and 1995 financial ratios, together with industry average data. The 1996 projected financial statement data represent Jamison's and Campo's best guess for 1996 results, assuming that some new financing is arranged to get the company "over the hump."

Jamison examined monthly data for 1995 (not given in the case), and she detected an improving pattern during the year. Monthly sales were rising, costs were falling, and large losses in the early months had turned to a small profit by December. Thus, the annual data look somewhat worse than final monthly data. Also, it appears to be taking longer for the advertising program to get the message across, for the new sales offices to generate sales, and for the new manufacturing facilities to operate efficiently. In other words, the lags between spending money and deriving benefits were longer than D'Leon's managers had anticipated. For these reasons, Jamison and Campo see hope for the company--provided it can survive in the short run.

Jamison must prepare an analysis of where the company is now, what it must do to regain its financial health, and what actions should be taken. Your assignment is to help her answer the following questions. Provide clear explanations, not yes or no answers.

Copyright © 1996 by The Dryden Press. All rights reserved.

Table IC3-1. Balance Sheets

	1996E	1995	1994
Assets:			
Cash	$ 85,632	$ 7,282	$ 57,600
Accounts receivable	878,000	632,160	351,200
Inventories	1,716,480	1,287,360	715,200
Total current assets	$2,680,112	$1,926,802	$1,124,000
Gross fixed assets	$1,197,160	$1,202,950	$ 491,000
Less accumulated depreciation	380,120	263,160	146,200
Net fixed assets	$ 817,040	$ 939,790	$ 344,800
Total assets	$3,497,152	$2,866,592	$1,468,800
Liabilities and Equity:			
Accounts payable	$ 436,800	$ 524,160	$ 145,600
Notes payable	600,000	720,000	200,000
Accruals	408,000	489,600	136,000
Total current liabilities	$1,444,800	$1,733,760	$ 481,600
Long-term debt	$ 500,000	$1,000,000	$ 323,432
Common stock	$1,680,936	$ 460,000	$ 460,000
Retained earnings	(128,584)	(327,168)	203,768
Total equity	$1,552,352	$ 132,832	$ 663,768
Total liabilities and equity	$3,497,152	$2,866,592	$1,468,800

Note: "E" indicates estimated. **The 1996 data are forecasts.**

Copyright © 1996 by The Dryden Press. All rights reserved.

Table IC3-2. Income Statements

	1996E	1995	1994
Sales	$7,035,600	$5,834,400	$3,432,000
Cost of goods sold	5,728,000	5,728,000	2,864,000
Other expenses	680,000	680,000	340,000
Depreciation	116,960	116,960	18,900
Total operating costs	$6,524,960	$6,524,960	$3,222,900
EBIT	$ 510,640	(690,560)	$ 209,100
Interest expense	88,000	176,000	62,500
EBT	$ 422,640	($ 866,560)	$ 146,600
Taxes (40%)	169,056	(346,624)	58,640
Net income	$ 253,584	($ 519,936)	$ 87,960
EPS	$1.014	($5.199)	$0.880
DPS	$0.220	$0.110	$0.220
Book value per share	$6.209	$1.328	$6.638
Stock price	$12.17	$2.250	$8.500
Shares outstanding	250,000	100,000	100,000
Tax rate	40.00%	40.00%	40.00%
Lease payments	40,000	40,000	40,000
Sinking fund payments	0	0	0

Note: "E" indicates estimated. The 1996 data are forecasts.

Copyright © 1996 by The Dryden Press. All rights reserved.

Table IC3-3. Ratio Analysis

	1996E	1995	1994	Industry Average
Current		1.1X	2.3X	2.7X
Quick		0.4X	0.8X	1.0X
Inventory turnover		4.5X	4.8X	6.1X
Days sales outstanding (DSO)		39.0	36.8	32.0
Fixed assets turnover		6.2X	10.0X	7.0X
Total assets turnover		2.0X	2.3X	2.6X
Debt ratio		95.4%	54.8%	50.0%
TIE		-3.9X	3.3X	6.2X
Fixed charge coverage		-3.0X	2.4X	5.1X
Profit margin		-8.9%	2.6%	3.5%
Basic earning power		-24.1%	14.2%	19.1%
ROA		-18.1%	6.0%	9.1%
ROE		-391.4%	13.3%	18.2%
Price/earnings		-0.4X	9.7X	14.2X
Market/book		1.7X	1.3X	2.4X
Book value per share		$1.33	$6.64	n.a.

Note: "E" indicates estimated. The 1996 data are forecasts.

a. Why are ratios useful? What are the five major categories of ratios?

b. Calculate D'Leon's 1996 current and quick ratios based on the projected balance sheet and income statement data. What can you say about the company's liquidity position in 1994, 1995, and as projected for 1996? We often think of ratios as being useful (1) to managers to help run the business, (2) to bankers for credit analysis, and (3) to stockholders for stock valuation. Would these different types of analysts have an equal interest in the liquidity ratios?

c. Calculate the 1996 inventory turnover, days sales outstanding (DSO), fixed assets turnover, and total assets turnover. How does D'Leon's utilization of assets stack up against other firms in its industry?

d. Calculate the 1996 debt, times-interest-earned, and fixed charge coverage ratios. How does D'Leon compare with the industry with respect to financial leverage? What can you conclude from these ratios?

Copyright © 1996 by The Dryden Press. All rights reserved.

e. Calculate the 1996 profit margin, basic earning power (BEP), return on assets (ROA), and return on equity (ROE). What can you say about these ratios?

f. Calculate the 1996 price/earnings ratio and market/book ratio. Do these ratios indicate that investors are expected to have a high or low opinion of the company?

g. Use the extended Du Pont equation to provide a summary and overview of D'Leon's financial condition as projected for 1996. What are the firm's major strengths and weaknesses?

h. Use the following simplified 1996 balance sheet to show, in general terms, how an improvement in the DSO would tend to affect the stock price. For example, if the company could improve its collection procedures and thereby lower its DSO from 44.9 days to the 32-day industry average without affecting sales, how would that change "ripple through" the financial statements (shown in thousands below) and influence the stock price?

Accounts receivable	$ 878	Debt	$1,945
Other current assets	1,802		
Net fixed assets	817	Equity	1,552
Total assets	$3,497	Liabilities plus equity	$3,497

i. Does it appear that inventories could be adjusted, and, if so, how should that adjustment affect D'Leon's profitability and stock price.

j. In 1995, the company paid its suppliers much later than the due dates, and it was not maintaining financial ratios at levels called for in its bank loan agreements. Therefore, suppliers could cut the company off, and its bank could refuse to renew the loan when it comes due in 90 days. Based on the data provided, would you, as a credit manager, continue to sell to D'Leon on credit? (You could demand cash on delivery, that is, sell on terms of COD, but that might cause D'Leon to stop buying from your company.) Similarly, if you were the bank loan officer, would you recommend renewing the loan or demand its repayment? Would your actions be influenced if, in early 1996, D'Leon showed you its 1996 projections plus proof that it was going to raise over $1.2 million of new equity capital?

k. In hindsight, what should D'Leon have done back in 1994?

Copyright © 1996 by The Dryden Press. All rights reserved.

CHAPTER 3
Analysis of Financial Statements

- Ratio Analysis
- Du Pont System
- Effects of Improving Ratios
- Limitations of Ratio Analysis

Balance Sheet: Assets

	1996E	1995
Cash	85,632	7,282
AR	878,000	632,160
Inventories	1,716,480	1,287,360
Total CA	2,680,112	1,926,802
Gross FA	1,197,160	1,202,950
Less: Deprec.	380,120	263,160
Net FA	817,040	939,790
Total assets	3,497,152	2,866,592

Liab. & Equity

	1996 (E)	1995
Accounts payable	436,800	524,160
Notes payable	600,000	720,000
Accruals	408,000	489,600
Total CL	1,444,800	1,733,760
Long-term debt	500,000	1,000,000
Common stock	1,680,936	460,000
Retained earnings	(128,584)	(327,168)
Total equity	1,552,352	132,832
Total L & E	3,497,152	2,866,592

BLUEPRINTS: CHAPTER 3

Copyright © 1996 by The Dryden Press. All rights reserved.

Income Statement

	1996E	1995
Sales	7,035,600	5,834,400
COGS	5,728,000	5,728,000
Other expenses	680,000	680,000
Depreciation	116,960	116,960
Tot. op. costs	6,524,960	6,524,960
EBIT	510,640	(690,560)
Interest exp.	88,000	176,000
EBT	422,640	(866,560)
Taxes (40%)	169,056	(346,624)
Net income	253,584	(519,936)

Other Data:

	1996E	1995
Shares out.	250,000	100,000
EPS	$1.014	($5.199)
DPS	$0.220	$0.110
Stock price	$12.17	$2.25
Lease pmts	$40,000	$40,000

Why are ratios useful?

- Standardize numbers; facilitate comparisons.

- Used to highlight weaknesses & strengths.

Copyright © 1996 by The Dryden Press. All rights reserved.

What are the five major categories of ratios, and what questions do they answer?

1. **Liquidity:** Can we make req'd payments?

2. **Asset mgt.:** Right amount of assets vs. sales?

3. **Debt mgt.:** Right mix of debt and equity?

4. **Profitability:** Do sales prices exceed unit costs, and are sales high enough, as reflected in PM, ROE, and ROA?

5. **Market values:** Do investors like what they see as reflected in P/E and M/B ratios?

Calculate D'Leon's forecasted current and quick ratios for 1996.

$$C.R_{96} = \frac{CA}{CL} = \frac{\$2,680}{\$1,445} = 1.85x.$$

$$Quick\ R_{96} = \frac{CA - Inv}{CL}$$

$$= \frac{\$2,680 - \$1,716}{\$1,445} = 0.67x.$$

Copyright © 1996 by The Dryden Press. All rights reserved.

Comments on CR and QR:

	1996	1995	1994	Ind.
CR	1.85x	1.1x	2.3x	2.7x
QR	0.67x	0.4x	0.8x	1.0x

- **Expected to improve but still below the industry average.**
- **Liquidity position is weak.**

What is the inventory turnover ratio vs. the industry average?

$$\text{Inv. turnover} = \frac{\text{Sales}}{\text{Inventories}}$$

$$= \frac{\$7,036}{\$1,716} = 4.10x.$$

	1996	1995	1994	Ind.
Inv.T.	4.1x	4.5x	4.8x	6.1x

Comment on Inv. Turnover:

- **Inv. turnover is below industry avg.**
- **D'Leon might have old inv., or its control might be poor.**
- **No improvement is currently forecasted.**

Copyright © 1996 by The Dryden Press. All rights reserved.

DSO is the average number of days after making a sale before receiving cash.

$$DSO = \frac{Receivables}{Average\ sales\ per\ day}$$

$$= \frac{Receivables}{Sales/360} = \frac{\$878}{\$7,036/360} = 44.9.$$

Appraisal of DSO:

	1996	1995	1994	Ind.
DSO	44.9	39.0	36.8	32.0

- **D'Leon collects too slowly, and is getting worse. Poor credit policy.**

F.A. and T.A. turnover vs. industry average

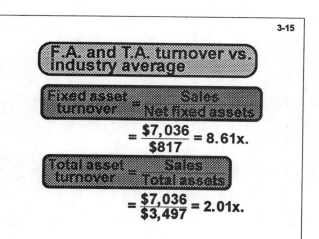

$$Fixed\ asset\ turnover = \frac{Sales}{Net\ fixed\ assets}$$

$$= \frac{\$7,036}{\$817} = 8.61x.$$

$$Total\ asset\ turnover = \frac{Sales}{Total\ assets}$$

$$= \frac{\$7,036}{\$3,497} = 2.01x.$$

Copyright © 1996 by The Dryden Press. All rights reserved.

	1996	1995	1994	Ind.
FA TO	8.6x	6.2x	10.0x	7.0x
TA TO	2.0x	2.0x	2.3x	2.6x

- **FA turnover projected to exceed ind. avg. Good.**

- **TA turnover not up to ind. avg. Caused by excessive current assets (A/R and inv.).**

Calculate the debt, TIE, and fixed charge coverage ratios.

$$\text{Debt ratio} = \frac{\text{Total debt}}{\text{Total assets}}$$

$$= \frac{\$1,445 + \$500}{\$3,497} = 55.6\%.$$

$$\text{TIE} = \frac{\text{EBIT}}{\text{Int. expense}} = \frac{\$510.6}{\$88} = 5.8x.$$

$$\frac{\text{Fixed charge}}{\text{coverage}} = \text{FCC}$$

$$= \frac{\text{EBIT + Lease payments}}{\text{Interest} + \text{Lease} + \frac{\text{Sinking fund pmt}}{(1-T)}}$$
$$\text{expense} \quad \text{pmt}$$

$$= \frac{\$510.6 + \$40}{\$88 + \$40 + \$0} = 4.3x.$$

All 3 ratios reflect use of debt, but focus on different aspects.

Copyright © 1996 by The Dryden Press. All rights reserved.

How do the debt mgt. ratios compare with industry avgs. ?

	1996	1995	1994	Ind.
D/A	55.6%	95.4%	54.8%	50.0%
TIE	5.8x	-3.9x	3.3x	6.2x
FCC	4.3x	-3.0x	2.4x	5.1x

Too much debt, but projected to improve.

Profit margin vs. industry average?

$$P.M. = \frac{NI}{Sales} = \frac{\$253.6}{\$7,036} = 3.6\%.$$

	1996	1995	1994	Ind.
P.M.	3.6%	-8.9%	2.8%	3.5%

Very bad in 1995, but projected to exceed ind. avg. in 1996. Looking good.

BEP vs. Ind. Avg.?

$$BEP = \frac{EBIT}{Total\ assets}$$

$$= \frac{\$510.6}{\$3,497} = 14.6\%.$$

Copyright © 1996 by The Dryden Press. All rights reserved.

	1996	1995	1994	Ind.
BEP	14.6%	-24.1%	14.2%	19.1%

- **BEP removes effects of taxes and financial leverage. Useful for comparisons.**
- **Projected to be below average.**
- **Room for improvement.**

Return on Assets

$$ROA = \frac{\text{Net income}}{\text{Total assets}}$$

$$= \frac{\$253.6}{\$3,497} = 7.3\%.$$

$$ROE = \frac{\text{Net income}}{\text{Common equity}}$$

$$= \frac{\$253.6}{\$1,552} = 16.3\%.$$

	1996	1995	1994	Ind.
ROA	7.3%	-18.1%	6.0%	9.1%
ROE	16.3%	-391%	13.3%	18.2%

Both below avg. but improving.

Copyright © 1996 by The Dryden Press. All rights reserved.

3-25

Effects of Debt on ROA and ROE:

- **ROA is lowered by debt -- interest lowers NI, which also lowers ROA = NI/Assets.**
- **But use of debt lowers equity, hence could raise ROE = NI/Equity.**

3-26

Calculate and appraise the P/E and M/B ratios.

Price = $12.17.

$$EPS = \frac{NI}{Shares\ out.} = \frac{\$253.6}{250} = \$1.01.$$

$$P/E = \frac{Price\ per\ share}{EPS} = \frac{\$12.17}{\$1.01} = 12x.$$

3-27

$$BVPS = \frac{Com.\ equity}{Shares\ out.}$$

$$= \frac{\$1,552}{250} = \$6.21.$$

$$M/B = \frac{Mkt.\ price\ per\ share}{Book\ value\ per\ share}$$

$$= \frac{\$12.17}{\$6.21} = 1.96x.$$

Copyright © 1996 by The Dryden Press. All rights reserved.

	1996	1995	1994	Ind.
P/E	12.0x	-0.4x	9.7x	14.2x
M/B	1.96x	1.7x	1.3x	2.4x

- P/E: How much investors will pay for $1 of earnings. High is good.
- M/B: How much paid for $1 of BV. Higher is good.
- P/E and M/B are high if ROE is high, risk is low.

Profit margin	T.A. turnover	Equity multiplier	= ROE
$\dfrac{NI}{Sales}$ x	$\dfrac{Sales}{TA}$ x	$\dfrac{TA}{CE}$	= ROE
1994	2.6%	x 2.3	x 2.2	= 13.2%
1995	-8.9%	x 2.0	x 21.9	= -391%
1996	3.6%	x 2.0	x 2.3	= 16.3%
Ind.	3.5%	x 2.6	x 2.0	= 18.2%

The Du Pont system focuses on:

- Expense control (P.M.)
- Asset utilization (TATO)
- Debt utilization (Eq. Mult.)

It shows how these factors combine to determine the ROE.

Copyright © 1996 by The Dryden Press. All rights reserved.

Simplified D'Leon Data:

A/R	878	Debt	1,945
Other CA	1,802	Equity	1,552
Net FA	817		
Total assets	$3,497	L&E	$3,497

$$\text{Sales}/\text{day} = \frac{\$7,035,600}{360} = \$19,543.$$

Q. How would reducing DSO to 32 days affect the company?

Effect of reducing DSO from 44.9 days to 32 days:

Old A/R = 19,543 x 44.9 = 878,000

New A/R = 19,543 x 32.0 = 625,376

Cash freed up: 252,624

Initially shows up as additional cash.

New Balance Sheet:

Added cash	$ 253	Debt	$1,945
A/R	625	Equity	1,552
Other CA	1,802		
Net FA	817		
Total assets	$3,497	Total L&E	$3,497

What could be done with the new cash? Affect on stock price and risk?

Copyright © 1996 by The Dryden Press. All rights reserved.

3-34

Potential uses of freed up cash:

- Reduce debt. Better debt ratio; lower interest, hence higher NI.

- Repurchase stock. Higher ROE, higher EPS.

- Expand business. Higher profits.

- All these actions would improve stock price.

3-35

Inventories are also too high.

Could analyze the effect of an inventory reduction on freeing up cash and increasing the quick ratio and asset management ratios--similar to what was done with DSO in Slides #31-#33.

3-36

Q. Would you lend money to the company?

A. Maybe. Things could get better. In business, one has to take some chances!

Copyright © 1996 by The Dryden Press. All rights reserved.

What are some potential problems and limitations of financial ratio analysis?

- Comparison with industry averages is difficult if the firm operates many different divisions.

- "Average" performance not necessarily good.

- Seasonal factors can distort ratios.

- "Window dressing" techniques can make statements and ratios look better.

- Different operating and accounting practices distort comparisons.

- Sometimes hard to tell if a ratio is "good" or "bad."

- Difficult to tell whether company is, on balance, in strong or weak position.

Copyright © 1996 by The Dryden Press. All rights reserved.

EXAM-TYPE PROBLEMS

1. Automotive Supply's ROE last year was only 2 percent, but its new owner has developed an operating plan designed to improve things. The new plan calls for a total debt ratio of 70 percent, which will result in interest charges of $500 per year. Management projects an EBIT of $2,000 on sales of $20,000, and it expects to have a total assets turnover ratio of 2.5. Under these conditions, the average tax rate will be 30 percent. If the changes are made, what return on equity will Automotive earn?

2. Capital Garden Supply (CGS) recently hired a new chief financial officer, Louise Johnston, who was brought in and charged with raising the firm's profitability. CGS has sales of $5 million, a profit margin of 5%, and the following balance sheet:

Cash	$ 250,000	A/P	$ 750,000
Receivables	2,250,000	Other C.L.	500,000
Inventories	1,750,000	Long-term debt	2,250,000
Net fixed assets	3,250,000	Common equity	4,000,000
Total assets	$7,500,000	Total L/E	$7,500,000

a. Ms. Johnston thinks that receivables are too high, and that they can be lowered to the point where the firm's DSO is equal to the industry average, 60 days, without affecting either sales or net income. If receivables are reduced so as to lower the DSO to 60 days (360-day basis), and if the funds generated are used to reduce common equity (stock can be repurchased at book value), and if no other changes occur, by how much will the ROE change?

b. Suppose we wanted to modify this problem and use it on an exam, i.e., to create a new problem which you have not seen to test your knowledge of this general type of problem. How would your answer change under each of the following conditions:

   (1)   Double all dollar amounts.

   (2)   Set the target DSO at 70 days.

   (3)   State that the target is to achieve a receivables turnover of 6x rather than a DSO of 60.

   (4)   State that the company has 250,000 shares of stock outstanding, and ask how much the original change would increase EPS.

   (5)   Change part 4 to state that the stock was selling for twice book value, so common equity would not be reduced on a dollar-for-dollar basis.

Copyright © 1996 by The Dryden Press. All rights reserved.

c. Now explain how we could have set the problem up to have you focus on changing inventory or fixed assets, or using the funds generated to retire debt, or how the original problem could have stated that the company needed *more* inventory and would finance them with new common equity, or with new debt.

3. Which of the following statements is most correct?

   a. If two firms pay the same interest rate on their debt and have the same rate of return on assets, and if that ROA is positive, the firm with the *higher* debt ratio will also have a higher rate of return on common equity.

   b. One of the problems of ratio analysis is that the relationships are subject to manipulation. For example, we know that if we use some of our cash to pay off some of our current liabilities, the current ratio will always increase, especially if the current ratio is weak initially.

   c. Generally, firms with high profit margins have high asset turnover ratios, and firms with low profit margins have low turnover ratios; this result is exactly as predicted by the extended Du Pont equation.

   d. Firms A and B have identical earnings and identical dividend payout ratios. If Firm A's growth rate is higher than that of Firm B, Firm A's P/E ratio must be greater than Firm B's P/E ratio.

   e. None of the above statements is correct.

4. Alumbat Corporation has $800,000 of debt outstanding, and it pays an interest rate of 10 percent annually on its bank loan. Alumbat's annual sales are $3,200,000; its average tax rate is 40 percent; and its net profit margin on sales is 6 percent. If the company does not maintain a TIE ratio of at least 4 times, its bank will refuse to renew its loan, and bankruptcy will result. What is Alumbat's current TIE ratio?

5. Austin & Company has a debt ratio of 0.5, a total assets turnover ratio of 0.25, and a profit margin of 10 percent. The Board of Directors is unhappy with the current return on equity (ROE), and they think it could be doubled. This could be accomplished (1) by increasing the profit margin to 12 percent, and (2) by increasing debt utilization. Total assets turnover will not change. What new debt ratio, along with the new 12 percent profit margin, would be required to double the ROE?

BLUEPRINTS: CHAPTER 3

Copyright © 1996 by The Dryden Press. All rights reserved.

4-11 Assume that you recently graduated with a degree in finance and have just reported to work as an investment advisor at the brokerage firm of Smyth Barry & Co. Your first assignment is to explain the nature of the U.S. financial markets to Michelle Varga, a professional tennis player who has just come to the United States from Mexico. Varga is a highly ranked tennis player who expects to invest substantial amounts of money through Smyth Barry. She is also very bright, and, therefore, she would like to understand in general terms what will happen to her money. Your boss has developed the following set of questions which you must ask and answer to explain the U.S. financial system to Varga.

a. What is a *market*? How are physical asset markets differentiated from financial markets?

b. Differentiate between *money markets* and *capital markets*.

c. Differentiate between a *primary market* and a *secondary market*. If Apple Computer decided to issue additional common stock, and Varga purchased 100 shares of this stock from Merrill Lynch, the underwriter, would this transaction be a primary market transaction or a secondary market transaction? Would it make a difference if Varga purchased previously outstanding Apple stock in the over-the-counter market?

d. Describe the three primary ways in which capital is transferred between savers and borrowers.

e. Securities can be traded on *organized exchanges* or in the *over-the-counter market*. Define each of these markets, and describe how stocks are traded in each of them.

f. What do we call the *price* that a borrower must pay for debt capital? What is the price of equity capital? What are the *four* most fundamental factors that affect the cost of money, or the general level of interest rates, in the economy?

g. What is the *real risk-free rate of interest (k*)* and the *nominal risk-free rate (k_{RF})*? How are these two rates measured?

Copyright © 1996 by The Dryden Press. All rights reserved.

h. Define the terms *inflation premium (IP)*, *default risk premium (DRP)*, *liquidity premium (LP)*, and *maturity risk premium (MRP)*. Which of these premiums is included when determining the interest rate on (1) short-term U.S. Treasury securities, (2) long-term U.S. Treasury securities, (3) short-term corporate securities, and (4) long-term corporate securities? Explain how the premiums would vary over time and among the different securities listed above.

i. What is the *term structure* of interest rates? What is a *yield curve*? At any given time, how would the yield curve facing a given company such as Exxon or Continental (whose bonds are classified as "junk bonds") compare with the yield curve for U.S. Treasury securities? Draw a graph to illustrate your answer.

j. Three theories have been advanced to explain the shape of the yield curve: (1) the *expectations theory*, (2) the *liquidity preference theory*, and (3) the *market segmentation theory*. Briefly describe each of these theories. Do economists regard one as being "true"?

k. Suppose most investors expect the rate of inflation to be 5 percent next year, 6 percent the following year, and 8 percent thereafter. The real risk-free rate is 3 percent. The maturity risk premium is zero for bonds that mature in 1 year or less, 0.1 percent for 2-year bonds, and then the MRP increases by 0.1 percent per year thereafter for 20 years, after which it is stable. What is the interest rate on 1-year, 10-year, and 20-year Treasury bonds? Draw a yield curve with these data. Is your yield curve consistent with the three term structure theories?

BLUEPRINTS: CHAPTER 4
Copyright © 1996 by The Dryden Press. All rights reserved.

CHAPTER 4
The Financial Environment:
Markets, Institutions,
and Interest Rates

- Financial Markets
- Types of Financial Institutions
- Determinants of Interest Rates
- Yield Curves

Define these markets:

1. Markets in general
2. Physical assets
3. Financial assets
4. Money vs. Capital
5. Primary vs. Secondary
6. Spot vs. Future

Three Primary Ways Capital is Transferred Between Savers and Borrowers:

- Direct Transfer
- Investment Banking House
- Financial Intermediary

Copyright © 1996 by The Dryden Press. All rights reserved.

Organized Exchanges vs. Over-the-Counter Market

- Auction Market vs. Dealer Market (Exchanges vs. OTC)
- NYSE vs. NASDAQ System
- Differences are Narrowing

- What do we call the price, or cost, of <u>debt</u> capital?

The interest rate

- What do we call the price, or cost, of <u>equity</u> capital?

$$\frac{\text{Required}}{\text{Return}} = \frac{\text{Dividend}}{\text{Yield}} + \frac{\text{Capital}}{\text{Gain}}$$

What four factors affect the cost of money?

- Production Opportunities
- Time Preferences for Consumption
- Risk
- Expected Inflation

Copyright © 1996 by The Dryden Press. All rights reserved.

"Real" versus "nominal" rates

k^* = <u>real</u> risk-free rate.
T-Bond rate if no inflation;
1% to 4%.

k = any <u>nominal</u> rate.

k_{RF} = Rate on T-securities.

$$k = k^* + IP + DRP + LP + MRP$$

Here:
k^* = Real risk - free rate
IP = Inflation premium
DRP = Default risk premium
LP = Liquidity premium
MRP = Maturity risk premium

Premiums Added to k^* for Different Types of Debt:

- S-T treasury: only IP for S-T infl.
- L-T treasury: IP for L-T infl., MRP
- S-T corporate: S-T IP, DRP, LP
- L-T corporate: IP, DRP, MRP, LP

BLUEPRINTS: CHAPTER 4

Copyright © 1996 by The Dryden Press. All rights reserved.

What is the "term structure of interest rates"? What is a "yield curve"?

- **Term structure:** the relationship between interest rates (or yields) and maturities.
- A graph of the term structure is called the **yield curve**.

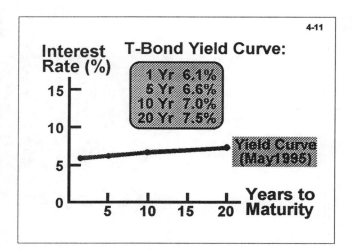

Interest Rate (%)

T-Bond Yield Curve:

1 Yr	6.1%
5 Yr	6.6%
10 Yr	7.0%
20 Yr	7.5%

Yield Curve (May 1995)

Years to Maturity

What 3 Theories Are Used to Explain the Shape of the Yield Curve?

Copyright © 1996 by The Dryden Press. All rights reserved.

1. Expectations:

- Shape of curve depends on investors' expectations about future inflation rates.
- If inflation is expected to increase, S-T rates will be low, L-T rates high, and vice versa. Thus, the yield curve can slope up or down.

2. Liquidity Preference:

- Lenders prefer S-T securities because they are less risky.
- Thus, S-T rates should be low, and the yield curve should be upward sloping.

3. Market Segmentation:

- Borrowers and lenders have preferred maturities.
- Slope of yield curve depends on supply and demand for funds in both the L-T and S-T markets (curve could be flat, upward, or downward sloping).

Copyright © 1996 by The Dryden Press. All rights reserved.

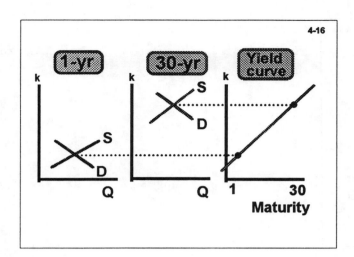

Example data:

- Inflation for Yr 1 is 5%.
- Inflation for Yr 2 is 6%.
- Inflation for Yr 3 and beyond is 8%.

  $k^* = 3\%$

  $MRP_t = 0.1\% \, (t - 1)$

Step 1: Find the average expected inflation rate over Years 1 to N:

$$IP_N = \frac{\sum_{t=1}^{N} INFL_t}{N}$$

Copyright © 1996 by The Dryden Press. All rights reserved.

$IP_1 = 5\%/1.0 = 5.00\%.$

$IP_{10} = [5 + 6 + 8(8)]/10 = 7.5\%.$

$IP_{20} = [5 + 6 + 8(18)]/20 = 7.75\%.$

Must earn these IPs to break even vs. inflation; these IPs would permit you to earn k* (before taxes).

Step 2: Find MRP based on this equation:

$$MRP_t = 0.1\%(t-1)$$

$MRP_1 = 0.1\% \times 0 = 0.0\%$

$MRP_{10} = 0.1\% \times 9 = 0.9\%$

$MRP_{20} = 0.1\% \times 19 = 1.9\%$

Step 3: Add the IPs and MRPs to k*:

$$k_{RF_t} = k^* + IP_t + MRP_t$$

k_{RF} = Quoted market interest rate on treasury securities

Assume k* = 3%:

1- Yr: $k_{RF_1} = 3\% + 5\% + 0.0\% = 8.0\%$

10 - Yr: $k_{RF_{10}} = 3\% + 7.5\% + 0.9\% = 11.4\%$

20 - Yr: $k_{RF_{20}} = 3\% + 7.75\% + 1.9\% = 12.7\%$

BLUEPRINTS: CHAPTER 4

Copyright © 1996 by The Dryden Press. All rights reserved.

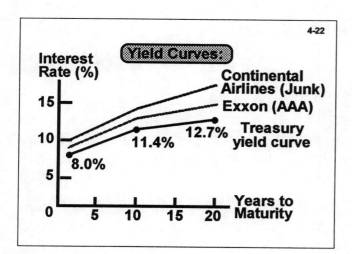

Copyright © 1996 by The Dryden Press. All rights reserved.

EXAM-TYPE PROBLEMS

1. Which of the following statements is most correct?

    a. If different markets existed for long-term and short-term bonds, but lenders and borrowers could move freely between markets, (1) the market segmentation theory could not really be an important determinant of the yield curve, and (2) maturity risk premiums could not be significant.

    b. Since the default risk premium (DRP) and the liquidity premium (LP) are both essentially zero for U.S. Treasury securities, the Treasury yield curve is influenced more heavily by expected inflation than corporate bonds' yield curves, i.e., we can be sure that a given amount of expected inflation will have more effect on the slope of the Treasury yield curve than on the corporate yield curve.

    c. According to the *market segmentation theory*, investors prefer to buy debt with short maturities. Therefore, the fundamental conclusion from this theory is that the yield curve should normally slope upwards.

    d. It is theoretically possible for the yield curve to have a downward slope, and there have been times when such a slope existed. That situation was probably caused by investors' liquidity preferences, i.e., by the factors which underlie the liquidity preference theory.

    e. Yield curves for government and corporate bonds can be constructed from data that exist in the marketplace. If the yield curves for several companies were plotted on a graph, along with the yield curve for U.S. Treasury securities, the company with the largest total of DRP plus LP would have the highest yield curve.

2. Assume that the real risk-free rate, k*, is 4 percent, and that inflation is expected to be 9% in Year 1, 6% in Year 2, and 4% thereafter. Assume also that all Treasury bonds are highly liquid and free of default risk. If 2-year and 5-year Treasury bonds both yield 12%, what is the difference in the maturity risk premiums (MRPs) on the two bonds, i.e., what is $MRP_5 - MRP_2$?

Copyright © 1996 by The Dryden Press. All rights reserved.

5-13 Assume that you recently graduated with a major in finance, and you just landed a job as a financial planner with Merrill Finch Inc., a large financial services corporation. Your first assignment is to invest $100,000 for a client. Because the funds are to be invested in a business at the end of one year, you have been instructed to plan for a one-year holding period. Further, your boss has restricted you to the following investment alternatives, shown with their probabilities and associated outcomes. (Disregard for now the items at the bottom of the data; you will fill in the blanks later.)

State of the Economy	Prob.	Returns on Alternative Investments					
		Estimated Rate of Return					
		T-Bills	High Tech	Collec-tions	U.S. Rubber	Market Portfolio	2-stock Portfolio
Recession	0.1	8.0%	-22.0%	28.0%	10.0%*	-13.0%	3.0%
Below avg	0.2	8.0	-2.0	14.7	-10.0	1.0	
Average	0.4	8.0	20.0	0.0	7.0	15.0	10.0%
Above avg	0.2	8.0	35.0	-10.0	45.0	29.0	
Boom	0.1	8.0	50.0	-20.0	30.0*	43.0	15.0
k-Hat ($\hat{k}$)				1.7%	13.8%	15.0%	
Std dev (σ)		0.0		13.4	18.8	15.3	3.3
Coef of var (CV)				7.9	1.4	1.0	0.3
Beta (b)				-0.86	0.68		

* Note that the estimated returns of U.S. Rubber do not always move in the same direction as the overall economy. For example, when the economy is below average, consumers purchase fewer tires than they would if the economy was stronger. However, if the economy is in a flat-out recession, a large number of consumers who were planning to purchase a new car may choose to wait and instead purchase new tires for the car they currently own. Under these circumstances, we would expect U.S. Rubber's stock price to be higher if there is a recession than if the economy was just below average.

Merrill Finch's economic forecasting staff has developed probability estimates for the state of the economy, and its security analysts have developed a sophisticated computer program which was used to estimate the rate of return on each alternative under each state of the economy. High Tech Inc. is an electronics firm; Collections Inc. collects past-due debts; and U.S. Rubber manufactures tires and various other rubber and plastics products. Merrill Finch also maintains an

Copyright © 1996 by The Dryden Press. All rights reserved.

"index fund" which owns a market-weighted fraction of all publicly traded stocks; you can invest in that fund, and thus obtain average stock market results. Given the situation as described, answer the following questions.

a. (1) Why is the T-bill's return independent of the state of the economy? Do T-bills promise a completely risk-free return?

   (2) Why are High Tech's returns expected to move with the economy whereas Collections' are expected to move counter to the economy?

b. Calculate the expected rate of return on each alternative and fill in the blanks on the row for $\hat{k}$ in the table above.

c. You should recognize that basing a decision solely on expected returns is only appropriate for risk-neutral individuals. Since your client, like virtually everyone, is risk averse, the riskiness of each alternative is an important aspect of the decision. One possible measure of risk is the *standard deviation* of returns.

   (1) Calculate this value for each alternative, and fill in the blank on the row for σ in the table above.

   (2) What type of risk is measured by the standard deviation?

   (3) Draw a graph which shows *roughly* the shape of the probability distributions for High Tech, U.S. Rubber, and T-bills.

d. Suppose you suddenly remembered that the *coefficient of variation (CV)* is generally regarded as being a better measure of stand-alone risk than the standard deviation when the alternatives being considered have widely differing expected returns. Calculate the missing CVs and fill in the blanks on the row for CV in the table above. Does the CV produce the same risk rankings as the standard deviation?

e. Suppose you created a 2-stock portfolio by investing $50,000 in High Tech and $50,000 in Collections.

   (1) Calculate the expected return $(\hat{k}_p)$, the standard deviation $_p(\sigma)$, and the coefficient of variation (CV_p) for this portfolio and fill in the appropriate blanks in the table above.

   (2) How does the riskiness of this 2-stock portfolio compare to the riskiness of the individual stocks if they were held in isolation?

Copyright © 1996 by The Dryden Press. All rights reserved.

f. Suppose an investor starts with a portfolio consisting of one randomly selected stock. What would happen (1) to the riskiness and (2) to the expected return of the portfolio as more and more randomly selected stocks were added to the portfolio? What is the implication for investors? Draw two graphs to illustrate your answer.

g. (1) Should portfolio effects impact the way investors think about the riskiness of individual stocks?

(2) If you decided to hold a 1-stock portfolio, and consequently were exposed to more risk than diversified investors, could you expect to be compensated for all of your risk; that is, could you earn a risk premium on that part of your risk that you could have eliminated by diversifying?

h. The expected rates of return and the beta coefficients of the alternatives as supplied by Merrill Finch's computer program are as follows:

Security	Return ($\hat{k}$)	Risk (Beta)
High Tech	17.4%	1.29
Market	15.0	1.00
U.S. Rubber	13.8	0.68
T-bills	8.0	0.00
Collections	1.7	(0.86)

(1) What is a *beta coefficient*, and how are betas used in risk analysis?

(2) Do the expected returns appear to be related to each alternative's market risk?

(3) Is it possible to choose among the alternatives on the basis of the information developed thus far? Use the data given at the start of the problem to construct a graph which shows how the T-bill's, High Tech's, and Collections' beta coefficients are calculated. Then discuss what betas measure and how they are used in risk analysis.

i. (1) Write out the Security Market Line (SML) equation, use it to calculate the required rate of return on each alternative, and then graph the relationship between the expected and required rates of return.

(2) How do the expected rates of return compare with the required rates of return?

(3) Does the fact that Collections has an expected return which is less than the T-bill rate make any sense?

Copyright © 1996 by The Dryden Press. All rights reserved.

(4)   What would be the market risk and the required return of a 50-50 portfolio of High Tech and Collections? Of High Tech and U.S. Rubber?

j.   (1)   Suppose investors raised their inflation expectations by 3 percentage points over current estimates as reflected in the 8 percent T-bill rate. What effect would higher inflation have on the SML and on the returns required on high- and low-risk securities?

     (2)   Suppose instead that investors' risk aversion increased enough to cause the market risk premium to increase by 3 percentage points. (Inflation remains constant.) What effect would this have on the SML and on returns of high- and low-risk securities?

Copyright © 1996 by The Dryden Press. All rights reserved.

CHAPTER 5
Risk and Rates of Return

- **Stand-alone Risk**
- **Portfolio Risk**
- **Risk & Return: CAPM/SML**

What is investment risk?

Investment risk pertains to the probability of earning less than the expected return.

The greater the chance of low or negative returns, the riskier the investment.

Copyright © 1996 by The Dryden Press. All rights reserved.

Investment Alternatives
(Given in the problem)

Economy	Prob.	T-Bill	HT	Coll	USR	MP
Recession	0.1	8.0%	-22.0%	28.0%	10.0%	-13.0%
Below avg.	0.2	8.0	-2.0	14.7	-10.0	1.0
Average	0.4	8.0	20.0	0.0	7.0	15.0
Above avg.	0.2	8.0	35.0	-10.0	45.0	29.0
Boom	0.1	8.0	50.0	-20.0	30.0	43.0
	1.0					

Why is the T-bill return independent of the economy?

Will return the promised 8% regardless of the economy.

Do T-bills promise a completely risk-free return?

No, T-bills are still exposed to the risk of inflation. However, not much <u>unexpected</u> inflation is likely to occur over a relatively short period.

Copyright © 1996 by The Dryden Press. All rights reserved.

Do the returns of HT and Coll. move with or counter to the economy?

- **HT:** With. Positive correlation. Typical.
- **Coll.** Countercyclical. Negative correlation. Unusual.

Calculate the expected rate of return on each alternative:

$\hat{k}$ = expected rate of return

$$\hat{k} = \sum_{i=1}^{n} k_i P_i$$

$$\hat{k}_{HT} = (-22\%)0.1 + (-2\%)0.20$$
$$+ (20\%)0.40 + (35\%)0.20$$
$$+ (50\%)0.1 = \boxed{17.4\%}$$

	$\hat{k}$
HT	17.4%
Market	15.0
USR	13.8
T-Bill	8.0
Coll.	1.7

HT appears to be the best, but is it really?

Copyright © 1996 by The Dryden Press. All rights reserved.

What's the standard deviation of returns for each alternative?

σ = standard deviation

$$s = \sqrt{\text{Variance}} = \sqrt{s^2}$$
$$= \sqrt{\sum_{i=1}^{n} (k_i - \hat{k})^2 P_i.}$$

$$\sigma = \sqrt{\sum_{i=1}^{n} \left(k_i - \hat{k}\right)^2 P_i.}$$

$$\sigma_{\text{T-bills}} = \left[\begin{array}{l} (8.0-8.0)^2 0.1 + (8.0-8.0)^2 0.20 \\ +(8.0-8.0)^2 0.4 + (8.0-8.0)^2 0.20 \\ +(8.0-8.0)^2 0.1 \end{array} \right]^{1/2}$$

$$= 0.0\%.$$

$$\sigma_{\text{HT}} = 20.0\%$$

$$\sigma_{\text{Coll}} = 13.4\%$$
$$\sigma_{\text{USR}} = 18.8\%$$
$$\sigma_M = 15.3\%$$

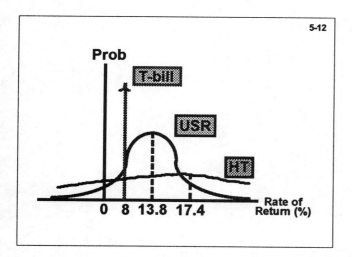

BLUEPRINTS: CHAPTER 5

Copyright © 1996 by The Dryden Press. All rights reserved.

- **Standard deviation** (σ_I) measures total, or <u>stand-alone</u>, risk.

- The larger the σ_I, the <u>lower</u> the probability that actual returns will be close to the expected return.

Expected Returns vs. Risk:

Security	Expected Return	Risk, σ
HT	17.4%	20.0
Market	15.0	15.3
USR	13.8*	18.8*
T-bills	8.0	0.0
Coll.	1.7*	13.4*

* Seems misplaced.

Coefficient of variation (CV)

Standardized measure of dispersion about the expected value:

$$CV = \frac{\text{Std dev}}{\text{Mean}} = \frac{\sigma}{\hat{k}}.$$

Shows risk per unit of return.

Copyright © 1996 by The Dryden Press. All rights reserved.

$\sigma_A = \sigma_B$, but A is riskier because larger prob. of losses.

$$\frac{\sigma}{\hat{k}} = CV_A > CV_B.$$

Portfolio Risk & Return

Assume a two-stock portfolio with \$50,000 in HT and \$50,000 in Collections.

Calculate $\hat{k}_p$ and σ_p.

Portfolio Return, $\hat{k}_p$

$\hat{k}_p$ is a weighted average:

$$\hat{k}_p = \sum_{i=1}^{n} w_i \hat{k}_i.$$

$\hat{k}_p = 0.5(17.4\%) + 0.5(1.7\%) = \boxed{9.6\%.}$

$\hat{k}_p$ is between $\hat{k}_{HT}$ and $\hat{k}_{COLL}$.

Copyright © 1996 by The Dryden Press. All rights reserved.

Alternative Method

Estimated Return

Economy	Prob.	HT	Coll.	Port.
Recession	0.10	-22.0%	28.0%	3.0%
Below avg.	0.20	-2.0	14.7	6.4
Average	0.40	20.0	0.0	10.0
Above avg.	0.20	35.0	-10.0	12.5
Boom	0.10	50.0	-20.0	15.0

$$\hat{k}_p = (3.0\%)0.1 + (6.4\%)0.20 + (10.0\%)0.4$$
$$+ (12.5\%)0.20 + (15.0\%)0.1 = 9.6\%.$$

$$\sigma_p = \begin{bmatrix} (3.0-9.6)^2 0.1 \\ +(6.4-9.6)^2 0.20 \\ +(10.0-9.6)^2 0.4 \\ +(12.5-9.6)^2 0.20 \\ +(15.0-9.6)^2 0.1 \end{bmatrix}^{1/2}$$

$$= \boxed{3.3\%.}$$

$$CV_p = \frac{3.3\%}{9.6\%} = \boxed{0.34.}$$

- $\sigma_p = 3.3\%$ is much lower than that of either stock (20% and 13.4%).

- $\sigma_p = 3.3\%$ is lower than avg. of HT and Coll = 16.7 %.

- ∴ Portfolio provides avg. $\hat{k}$ but lower risk.

- Reason: Negative correlation.

Copyright © 1996 by The Dryden Press. All rights reserved.

General statements about risk:

- **Most stocks are positively correlated.** $r_{k,M} \approx 0.65$.

- $\sigma \approx 35\%$ for an average stock.

- **Combining stocks generally lowers risk.**

Returns Distributions for Two Perfectly Negatively Correlated Stocks (r = -1.0) and for Portfolio WM:

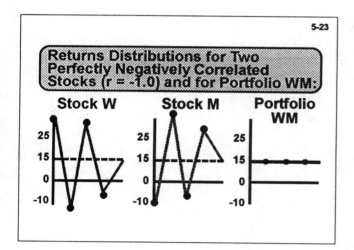

Returns Distributions for Two Perfectly Positively Correlated Stocks (r = +1.0) and for Portfolio MM':

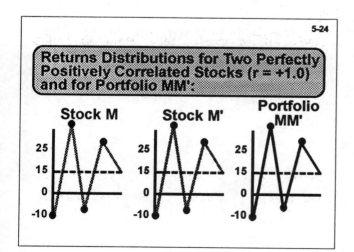

Copyright © 1996 by The Dryden Press. All rights reserved.

What would happen to the riskiness of a 1-stock portfolio as more randomly selected stocks were added?

- σ_p would decrease because the added stocks would not be perfectly correlated but $\hat{k}_p$ would remain constant.

Even with large N, $\sigma_p \approx 20\%$.

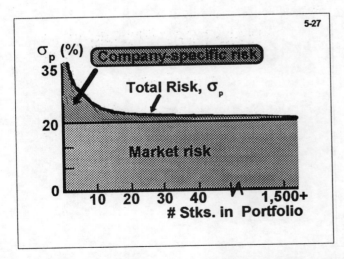

Copyright © 1996 by The Dryden Press. All rights reserved.

- As more stocks are added, each new stock has a smaller risk-reducing impact.

- σ_p falls very slowly after about 40 stocks are included. The lower limit for σ_p is about 20% = σ_M.

$$\text{Total} = \text{Market} + \text{Firm-specific}$$
$$\text{risk} \quad \text{risk} \quad \text{risk}$$

Market risk is that part of a security's risk that *cannot* be eliminated by diversification.

Firm-specific risk is that part of a security's risk which can be eliminated by proper diversification.

- By forming portfolios, we can eliminate about half the riskiness of individual stocks (35% vs. 20%).

BLUEPRINTS: CHAPTER 5

Copyright © 1996 by The Dryden Press. All rights reserved.

If you chose to hold a one-stock portfolio and thus are exposed to more risk than diversified investors, would you be compensated for all the risk you bear?

- NO!
- Stand-alone risk as measured by a stock's σ or CV is not important to a well-diversified investor.
- Rational, risk averse investors are concerned with σ_P, which is based on market risk.

- There can be only one price, hence market return, for a given security. Therefore, no compensation can be earned for the additional risk of a one-stock portfolio.

Copyright © 1996 by The Dryden Press. All rights reserved.

- Beta measures a stock's market risk. It shows a stock's volatility relative to the market.

- Beta shows how risky a stock is if the stock is held in a well-diversified portfolio.

How are betas calculated?

- Run a regression of past returns on Stock *i* versus returns on the market. Returns = D/P + g.

- The slope coefficient of the regression line is defined as the beta coefficient.

Illustration of beta calculations:

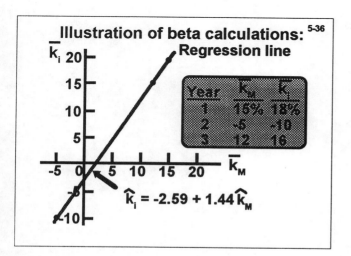

$\hat{k}_i = -2.59 + 1.44 \hat{k}_M$

BLUEPRINTS: CHAPTER 5

Copyright © 1996 by The Dryden Press. All rights reserved.

Find beta.

1. **"By Eye."** Plot points, draw in regression line, set slope as b = Rise/Run. The "rise" is the difference in k_I, the "run" is the difference in k_M, e.g., how much does k_I increase or decrease when k_M increases from 0% to 10%?

2. **Calculator.** Enter data points, and calculator does least squares regression: $k_I = a + bk_M = -2.59 + 1.44k_M$. r = corr. coefficient = 0.997.

3. In the real world, we would use **weekly or monthly returns**, with at least a year of data, and would always use a computer or calculator.

- If beta = 1.0, average stock.
- If beta > 1.0, stock riskier than average.
- If beta < 1.0, stock less risky than average.
- Most stocks have betas in the range of 0.5 to 1.5.

Copyright © 1996 by The Dryden Press. All rights reserved.

Can a beta be negative?

Answer: Yes, if $r_{I,M}$ is negative. Then in a "beta graph" the regression line will slope downward.

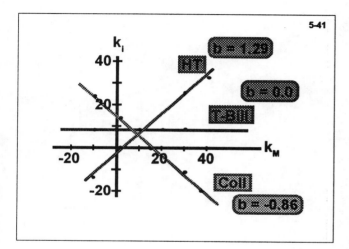

Security	Expected Return	Risk (Beta)
HT	17.4%	1.29
"Market"	15.0	1.00
USR	13.8	0.68
T-bills	8.0	0.00
Coll.	1.7	-0.86

Riskier securities have higher returns, so the rank order is O.K.

Copyright © 1996 by The Dryden Press. All rights reserved.

Use the SML to calculate the required returns.

$$\text{SML: } k_i = k_{RF} + (k_M - k_{RF})b_i.$$

- Assume $k_{RF} = 8\%$.
- Note that $k_M = \hat{k}_M$ is 15%. (Equil.)
- $RP_M = k_M - k_{RF} = 15\% - 8\% = 7\%$.

Required rates of return:

$$
\begin{aligned}
k_{HT} &= 8.0\% + (15.0\% - 8.0\%)1.29 \\
&= 8.0\% + (7\%)1.29 \\
&= 8.0\% + 9.0\% = 17.0\% \\
k_M &= 8.0\% + (7\%)1.00 = 15.0\% \\
k_{USR} &= 8.0\% + (7\%)0.68 = 12.8\% \\
k_{T\text{-}bills} &= 8.0\% + (7\%)0.00 = 8.0\% \\
k_{Coll} &= 8.0\% + (7\%)(-0.86) = 2.0\%
\end{aligned}
$$

Expected vs. Required Returns

	$\hat{k}$	k	
HT	17.4%	17.0%	Underval: $\hat{k} > k$
Market	15.0	15.0	Fairly valued
USR	13.8	12.8	Underval: $\hat{k} > k$
T-bills	8.0	8.0	Fairly valued
Coll.	1.7	2.0	Overvalued $\hat{k} < k$

Copyright © 1996 by The Dryden Press. All rights reserved.

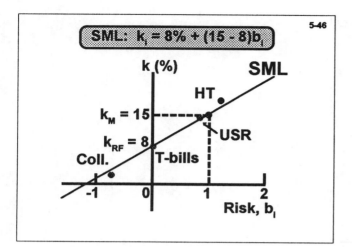

SML: $k_i = 8\% + (15 - 8)b_i$

Calculate beta for a portfolio with 50% HT and 50% Collections:

b_p = Weighted average

$\quad = 0.5(b_{HT}) + 0.5(b_{Coll})$

$\quad = 0.5(1.29) + 0.5(-0.86)$

$\quad = \boxed{0.22}$.

The required return on the HT/Coll. portfolio is:

k_p = Weighted average k

$\quad = 0.5(17\%) + 0.5(2\%) = \boxed{9.5\%}$.

Or use SML:

$k_p = k_{RF} + (k_M - k_{RF})b_p$

$\quad = 8.0\% + (15.0\% - 8.0\%)(0.22)$

$\quad = 8.0\% + 7\%(0.22) \quad = \boxed{9.5\%}$.

BLUEPRINTS: CHAPTER 5

Copyright © 1996 by The Dryden Press. All rights reserved.

If investors raise inflation expectations by 3%, what would happen to the SML?

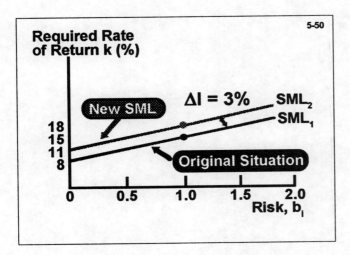

Required Rate of Return k (%)

New SML $\Delta I = 3\%$ SML$_2$

SML$_1$

18
15
11
8

Original Situation

0   0.5   1.0   1.5   2.0

Risk, b$_i$

If inflation did not change but risk aversion increased enough to cause the market risk premium to increase by 3 percentage points, what would happen to the SML?

Copyright © 1996 by The Dryden Press. All rights reserved.

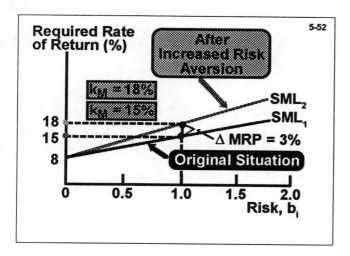

Required Rate of Return (%)

After Increased Risk Aversion

$k_M = 18\%$
$k_M = 15\%$

SML₂
SML₁

18
15
8

Δ MRP = 3%

Original Situation

0   0.5   1.0   1.5   2.0
Risk, b_i

Has the CAPM been verified through empirical tests?

- Not completely. The statistical tests have problems which make verification almost impossible.

- Investors seem to be concerned with both market risk and total risk. Therefore, the SML may not produce a correct estimate of k_i:

$$k_i = k_{RF} + (k_M - k_{RF})b + ?$$

BLUEPRINTS: CHAPTER 5

Copyright © 1996 by The Dryden Press. All rights reserved.

5-55

■ Also, CAPM/SML concepts
are based on expectations,
yet betas are calculated
using historical data. A
company's historical data
may not reflect investors'
expectations about future
riskiness.

Copyright © 1996 by The Dryden Press. All rights reserved.

EXAM-TYPE PROBLEMS

1. For markets to be in equilibrium (that is, for there to be no strong pressure for prices to depart from their current levels),

   a. The expected rate of return must be equal to the required rate of return; that is, $\hat{k}$ = k.

   b. The past realized rate of return must be equal to the expected rate of return; that is, $\bar{k} = \hat{k}$.

   c. The required rate of return must equal the realized rate of return; that is, $k = \bar{k}$.

   d. All three of the above statements must hold for equilibrium to exist; that is, $\hat{k} = k = \bar{k}$.

   e. None of the above statements is correct.

2. Which of the following statements is most correct?

   a. According to CAPM theory, the required rate of return on a given stock can be found by use of the SML equation:

   $$k_i = k_{RF} + (k_M - k_{RF})b_i.$$

   Expectations for inflation are not reflected anywhere in this equation, even indirectly, and because of that the text notes that the CAPM may not be strictly correct.

   b. If the required rate of return is given by the SML equation as set forth in *answer a*, there is nothing a financial manager can do to change his or her company's cost of capital, because each of the elements in the equation is determined exclusively by the market, not by the type of actions a company's management can take, even in the long run.

   c. Assume that the required rate of return on the market is currently k_M = 15%, and that k_M remains fixed at that level. If the yield curve has a steep upward slope, the calculated market risk premium would be larger if the 30-day T-bill rate were used as the risk-free rate than if the 30-year T-bond rate were used as k_{RF}.

   d. Statements a and b are both true.

   e. Statements a and c are both true.

Copyright © 1996 by The Dryden Press. All rights reserved.

3. You hold a diversified portfolio consisting of a $5,000 investment in each of 20 different common stocks. The portfolio beta is equal to 1.15. You have decided to sell one of your stocks, a lead mining stock whose b = 1.0, for $5,000 net and to use the proceeds to buy $5,000 of stock in a steel company whose b = 2.0. What will be the new beta of the portfolio?

Copyright © 1996 by The Dryden Press. All rights reserved.

BLUEPRINTS: CHAPTER 6
TIME VALUE OF MONEY

6-36 Assume that you are nearing graduation and that you have applied for a job with a local bank, First National Bank. As part of the bank's evaluation process, you have been asked to take an examination which covers several financial analysis techniques. The first section of the test addresses time value of money analysis. See how you would do by answering the following questions.

a. Draw time lines for (a) a $100 lump sum cash flow at the end of year 2, (b) an ordinary annuity of $100 per year for 3 years, and (c) an uneven cash flow stream of -$50, $100, $75, and $50 at the end of Years 0 through 3.

b. (1) What is the future value of an initial $100 after 3 years if it is invested in an account paying 10 percent, annual compounding?

 (2) What is the present value of $100 to be received in 3 years if the appropriate interest rate is 10 percent, annual compounding?

c. We sometimes need to find how long it will take a sum of money (or anything else) to grow to some specified amount. For example, if a company's sales are growing at a rate of 20 percent per year, how long will it take sales to double?

d. What is the difference between an ordinary annuity and an annuity due? What type of annuity is shown below? How would you change it to the other type of annuity?

e. (1) What is the future value of a 3-year ordinary annuity of $100 if the appropriate interest rate is 10 percent, annual compounding?

 (2) What is the present value of the annuity?

 (3) What would the future and present values be if the annuity were an annuity due?

Copyright © 1996 by The Dryden Press. All rights reserved.

f. What is the present value of the following uneven cash flow stream? The appropriate interest rate is 10 percent, compounded annually.

```
0        1        2        3        4  Years
├────────┼────────┼────────┼────────┤
0       100      300      300      -50
```

g. What annual interest rate will cause $100 to grow to $125.97 in 3 years?

h. (1) Will the future value be larger or smaller if we compound an initial amount more often than annually, for example, every 6 months, or *semiannually*, holding the stated interest rate constant? Why?

    (2) Define (a) the *stated, or quoted, or nominal, rate*, (b) the *periodic rate*, and (c) the *effective annual rate (EAR)*.

    (3) What is the effective annual rate corresponding to a nominal rate of 10 percent, compounded semiannually? Compounded quarterly? Compounded daily?

    (4) What is the future value of $100 after 3 years under 10 percent semiannual compounding? Quarterly compounding?

i. When will the effective annual rate be equal to the nominal (quoted) rate?

j. (1) What is the value at the end of Year 3 of the following cash flow stream if the quoted interest rate is 10 percent, compounded semiannually?

```
0        2        4        6  Periods
├────┼────┼────┼────┼────┼────┤
    100      100      100
```

    (2) What is the PV of the same stream?

    (3) Is the stream an annuity?

    (4) An important rule is that you should *never* show a nominal rate on a time line or use it in calculations unless what condition holds? (Hint: Think of annual compounding, when $i_{Nom} = EAR = i_{PER}$.) What would be wrong with your answer to questions j(1) and j(2) if you used the nominal rate, 10 percent, rather than the periodic rate $i_{Nom}/2 = 10\%/2 = 5\%$?

k. (1) Construct an amortization schedule for a $1,000, 10 percent, annual compounding, loan with 3 equal installments.

Copyright © 1996 by The Dryden Press. All rights reserved.

(2) What is the annual interest expense for the borrower, and the annual interest income for the lender, during Year 2?

l. Suppose on January 1, 1995, you deposit $100 in an account that pays a nominal, or quoted, interest rate of 10 percent, with interest added (compounded) 365 times per year. How much would you have in your account on October 1, or after 9 months (273 days)?

m. Now, suppose you left your money in the bank for 21 months. Thus, on January 1, 1995, you deposit $100 in an account that pays 10 percent, daily compounding, with a 365-day year. How much would be in your account on October 1, 1996, or 273 + 365 = 638 days later?

n. Suppose someone offered to sell you a note calling for the payment of $1,000 15 months from today (456 days). They offer to sell it to you for $850. You have $850 in a bank time deposit which pays a 7.0 percent nominal rate with daily (365 days per year) compounding, and you plan to leave the money in the bank unless you buy the note. The note is not risky--you are sure it will be paid on schedule. Should you buy the note? Check the decision in three ways: (1) by comparing your future value if you buy the note versus leaving your money in the bank, (2) by comparing the PV of the note with your current bank account, and (3) by comparing the EAR on the note versus that of the bank account.

o. Suppose the note discussed in Part n had a cost of $850, but called for 5 quarterly payments of $190 each, with the first payment due in 3 months rather than $1,000 at the end of 15 months. Would it be a good investment for you? (Assume that today is January 1, 1995, and that the first payment will be due April 1, 1995.)

Copyright © 1996 by The Dryden Press. All rights reserved.

6-1

CHAPTER 6
Time Value of Money

- **Future Value**
- **Present Value**
- **Rates of Return**
- **Amortization**

6-2

- **Time lines** show timing of cash flows.

```
0        1        2        3
|   I%   |        |        |
CF₀      CF₁      CF₂      CF₃
```

- **Tick marks** at ends of periods, so Time 0 is today; Time 1 is the end of Period 1, or the beginning of Period 2.

6-3

A. (1) a. Time line for a $100 lump sum due at the end of Year 2.

```
0     I%    1         2   Year
|----------|----------|
                     100
```

Copyright © 1996 by The Dryden Press. All rights reserved.

A. (1) b. Time line for an ordinary annuity of $100 for 3 years.

A. (1) c. Time line for uneven CFs -$50 at t = 0 and $100, $75, and $50 at the end of Years 1 through 3.

What's the FV of an initial $100 after 3 years if i = 10%?

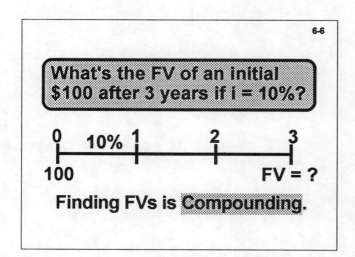

Finding FVs is Compounding.

Copyright © 1996 by The Dryden Press. All rights reserved.

After 1 year:

$$FV_1 = PV + I_1 = PV + PV(i)$$
$$= PV(1 + i)$$
$$= \$100(1.10) = \$110.00.$$

After 2 years:

$$FV_2 = PV(1 + i)^2$$
$$= \$100(1.10)^2 = \$121.00.$$

After 3 years:

$$FV_3 = PV(1 + i)^3$$
$$= 100(1.10)^3 = \$133.10.$$

In general,

$$FV_n = PV(1 + i)^n$$

Three ways to find FVs:

1. **Solve the Equation With a Regular Calculator**

2. **Use Tables**

3. **Use a Financial Calculator**

BLUEPRINTS: CHAPTER 6

Copyright © 1996 by The Dryden Press. All rights reserved.

Financial Calculator Solution:

Financial calculators solve this equation:

$$FV_n = PV(1+i)^n.$$

There are 4 variables. If 3 are known, the calculator will solve for the 4th.

Here's the setup to find FV:

INPUTS	3	10	-100	0	
	(N)	(I/YR)	(PV)	(PMT)	(FV)
OUTPUT					133.10

Clearing automatically sets everything to 0, but for safety enter PMT = 0.

Set: P/YR = 1, END

What's the PV of $100 due in 3 years if i = 10%?

Finding PVs is <u>discounting</u>, and it's the reverse of compounding.

PV = ?

Copyright © 1996 by The Dryden Press. All rights reserved.

Solve $FV_n = PV(1+i)^n$ for PV:

$$PV = \frac{FV_n}{(1+i)^n} = FV_n\left(\frac{1}{1+i}\right)^n$$

$$PV = \$100\left(\frac{1}{1.10}\right)^3 = \$100(PVIF_{i,n})$$
$$= \$100(0.7513) = \$75.13.$$

Financial Calculator Solution:

INPUTS	3	10		0	100
	N	I/YR	PV	PMT	FV
OUTPUT			-75.13		

Either PV or FV must be negative. Here PV = -75.13. Put in $75.13 today, take out $100 after 3 years.

If sales grow at 20% per year, how long before sales double?

Solve for n:

$$FV_n = 1(1+i)^n;$$
$$2 = 1(1.20)^n.$$

Copyright © 1996 by The Dryden Press. All rights reserved.

Graphical Illustration:

What's the difference between an _ordinary annuity_ and an _annuity due_?

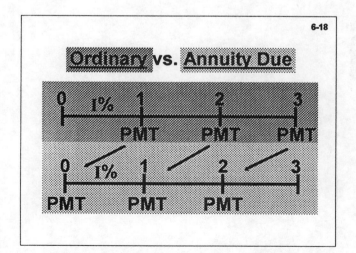

Ordinary vs. Annuity Due

BLUEPRINTS: CHAPTER 6

Copyright © 1996 by The Dryden Press. All rights reserved.

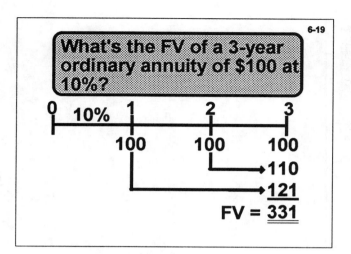

What's the FV of a 3-year ordinary annuity of $100 at 10%?

0   10%   1   2   3

100   100   100

→ 110

→ 121

FV = 331

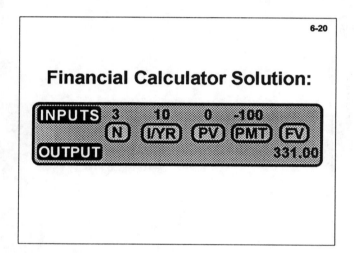

Financial Calculator Solution:

INPUTS	3	10	0	-100	
	N	I/YR	PV	PMT	FV
OUTPUT					331.00

What's the PV of this ordinary annuity?

0   10%   1   2   3

100   100   100

90.91 ←

82.64 ←

75.13 ←

248.69 = PV

Copyright © 1996 by The Dryden Press. All rights reserved.

Financial Calculator Solution:

INPUTS	3	10		100	0
	(N)	(I/YR)	(PV)	(PMT)	(FV)
OUTPUT			-248.69		

Have payments but no lump sum FV, so enter 0 for future value.

6-22

6-23

Find the FV and PV if the annuity were an annuity due.

6-24

Switch from "End" to "Begin".

Then enter variables to find PVA$_3$ = $273.55.

INPUTS	3	10		100	0
	(N)	(I/YR)	(PV)	(PMT)	(FV)
OUTPUT			-273.55		

Then enter PV = 0 and press FV to find FV = $364.10.

BLUEPRINTS: CHAPTER 6

Copyright © 1996 by The Dryden Press. All rights reserved.

Slide 6-25

What is the PV of this uneven cash flow stream?

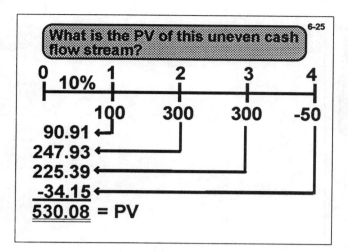

```
 0    10%   1        2        3        4
 |----------|--------|--------|--------|
           100      300      300      -50
 90.91 ←
247.93 ←─────────────
225.39 ←──────────────────────
-34.15 ←───────────────────────────────
530.08 = PV
```

Slide 6-26

- **Input in 'CFLO" register:**
  $CF_0 = 0$
  $CF_1 = 100$
  $CF_2 = 300$
  $CF_3 = 300$
  $CF_4 = -50$
- **Enter I = 10%, then press NPV button to get NPV = 530.09. (Here NPV = PV.)**

Slide 6-27

What interest rate would cause $100 to grow to $125.97 in 3 years?

$$\$100(1+i)^3 = \$125.97.$$

INPUTS	3		-100	0	125.97
	N	I/YR	PV	PMT	FV
OUTPUT		8%			

BLUEPRINTS: CHAPTER 6

Copyright © 1996 by The Dryden Press. All rights reserved.

Will the FV of a lump sum be larger or smaller if we compound more often, holding the stated I% constant? Why?

Larger! If compounding is more frequent than once a year--for example, semiannually, quarterly, or daily--interest is earned on interest more often.

Annually: $FV_3 = 100 (1.10)^3 = 133.10.$

Semiannually:

$FV_{6/2} = 100 (1.05)^6 = 134.01.$

We will deal with 3 different rates:

i_{Nom} = nominal, or stated, or quoted, rate per year.

i_{Per} = periodic rate.

EAR = EFF% = effective annual rate.

Copyright © 1996 by The Dryden Press. All rights reserved.

- i_{Nom} is stated in contracts. Periods per year (m) must also be given.

- Examples:

  8%, Quarterly

  8%, Daily interest (365 days)

- <u>Periodic rate</u> = $i_{Per} = i_{Nom}/m$, where m is periods per year. m = 4 for quarterly, 12 for monthly, and 360 or 365 for daily compounding.

- Examples:

  8% quarterly: i_{per} = 8/4 = 2%

  8% daily (365): i_{per} = 8/365

  $\qquad\qquad$ = 0.021918%

- <u>Effective Annual Rate</u> (EAR = EFF%): The annual rate which causes PV to grow to the same FV as under multiperiod compounding.

  Example: EFF% for 10%, semiannual:

  $FV = (1 + i_{Nom}/m)^m$

  $\qquad = (1.05)^2 = 1.1025.$

  EFF% = 10.25% because

  $\qquad (1.1025)^1 = 1.1025.$

  Any PV would grow to same FV at 10.25% annually or 10% semiannually.

Copyright © 1996 by The Dryden Press. All rights reserved.

- **An investment with monthly payments is different from one with quarterly payments. Must put on EFF% basis to compare rates of return. Use EFF% only for comparisons.**

- **Banks say "interest paid daily". Same as compounded daily.**

How do we find EFF% for a nominal rate of 10%, compounded semiannually?

$$EFF\% = \left(1 + \frac{i_{Nom}}{m}\right)^m - 1.$$

$$= \left(1 + \frac{0.10}{2}\right)^2 - 1.0$$

$$= (1.05)^2 - 1.0$$

$$= 0.1025 = 10.25\%.$$

Or use a financial calculator.

EAR = EFF% of 10%

$EAR_{Annual} = \boxed{10\%.}$

$EAR_Q = (1 + 0.10/4)^4 - 1$
$\qquad\qquad = \boxed{10.38\%.}$

$EAR_M = (1 + 0.10/12)^{12} - 1$
$\qquad\qquad = \boxed{10.47\%.}$

$EAR_D = (1 + 0.10/360)^{360} - 1$
$\qquad\qquad = \boxed{10.52\%.}$

Copyright © 1996 by The Dryden Press. All rights reserved.

Can the effective rate ever be equal to the nominal rate?

- **Yes**, but only if annual compounding is used, i.e., if **m = 1**.

- **If m > 1**, EFF% will always be **greater** than the nominal rate.

When is each rate used?

 Written into contracts, quoted by banks and brokers. _Not_ used in calculations or shown on time lines.

 Used in calculations, shown on time lines.

If i_{Nom} has annual compounding, then $i_{Per} = i_{Nom}/1 = i_{Nom}$.

Copyright © 1996 by The Dryden Press. All rights reserved.

EAR = EFF% Used to compare returns on investments with different payments per year.

(Used for calculations if and only if dealing with annuities where payments don't match interest compounding periods.)

FV of $100 after 3 years under 10% semiannual compounding? Quarterly?

$$FV_n = PV\left(1 + \frac{i_{Nom}}{m}\right)^{mn}.$$

$$FV_{3S} = \$100\left(1 + \frac{0.10}{2}\right)^{2 \times 3}$$

$$= \$100(1.05)^6 = \$134.01.$$

$$FV_{3Q} = \$100(1.025)^{12} = \$134.49.$$

What's the value at the end of Year 3 of the following CF stream if the quoted interest rate is 10%, compounded semiannually?

6-month periods

```
0   5% 1    2    3    4    5    6
|------|----|----|----|----|----|
          100  100  100
```

Copyright © 1996 by The Dryden Press. All rights reserved.

- **Payments occur annually, but compounding occurs each 6 months.**

- **So, we can't use normal annuity valuation techniques.**

1st Method: Compound each CF

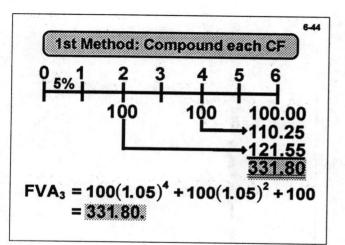

$$FVA_3 = 100(1.05)^4 + 100(1.05)^2 + 100$$
$$= 331.80.$$

2nd Method: Treat as an Annuity

Could you find FV with a financial calculator?

Yes, by following these steps:

a. Find the EAR for the quoted rate:

$$EAR = \left(1 + \frac{0.10}{2}\right)^2 - 1 = 10.25\%.$$

BLUEPRINTS: CHAPTER 6

Copyright © 1996 by The Dryden Press. All rights reserved.

Or, to find EAR with a calculator:

NOM% = 10

P/YR = 2

EFF% = 10.25

b. The cash flow stream is an annual annuity. Find k_{Nom} (annual) whose EFF% = 10.25. In calculator,

EFF% = 10.25

P/YR = 1

NOM% = 10.25

c.

INPUTS	3	10.25	0	-100	
	N	I/YR	PV	PMT	FV
OUTPUT					331.80

What's the PV of this stream?

Years

```
  0   5%    1        2        3
  |---------|--------|--------|
           100      100      100
90.70 ←
82.27 ←
74.62 ←
247.59
```

Copyright © 1996 by The Dryden Press. All rights reserved.

AMORTIZATION

Construct an amortization schedule for a $1,000, 10% annual rate loan with 3 equal payments.

Step 1: Find the required payments.

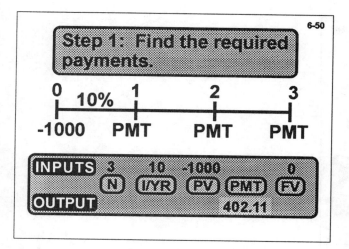

Step 2: Find interest charge for Year 1.

$$INT_t = Beg\ bal_t(i)$$
$$INT_1 = 1,000(0.10) = \boxed{\$100.}$$

Step 3: Find repayment of principal in Year 1.

$$Repmt. = PMT - INT$$
$$= 402.11 - 100$$
$$= \boxed{\$302.11.}$$

Copyright © 1996 by The Dryden Press. All rights reserved.

Step 4: Find ending balance after Year 1.

End bal = Beg bal - Repmt

$= 1,000 - 302.11 = \$697.89$.

Repeat these steps for Years 2 and 3 to complete the amortization table.

YR	BEG BAL	PMT	INT	PRIN PMT	END BAL
1	$1,000	$402	$100	$302	$698
2	698	402	70	332	366
3	366	402	37	366	0
TOT		1,206.34	206.34	1,000	

Interest declines. Tax implications.

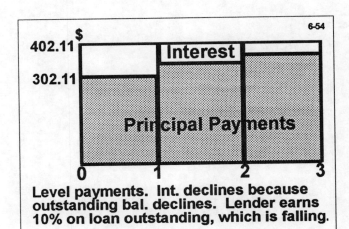

Level payments. Int. declines because outstanding bal. declines. Lender earns 10% on loan outstanding, which is falling.

Copyright © 1996 by The Dryden Press. All rights reserved.

- Amortization tables are widely used--for home mortgages, auto loans, business loans, retirement plans, etc. They are very important!

- Financial calculators (and spreadsheets) are great for setting up amortization tables.

On Jan. 1 you deposit $100 in an account that pays a nominal interest rate of 10%, with daily compounding (365 days).

How much will you have on October 1, or after 9 months (273 days)? (Days given.)

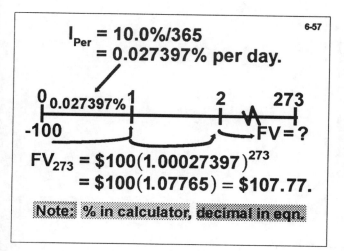

$$I_{Per} = 10.0\%/365$$
$$= 0.027397\% \text{ per day.}$$

$$FV_{273} = \$100(1.00027397)^{273}$$
$$= \$100(1.07765) = \$107.77.$$

Note: % in calculator, decimal in eqn.

Copyright © 1996 by The Dryden Press. All rights reserved.

$$i_{Per} = i_{Nom} / m$$
$$= 10.0 / 365$$
$$= 0.027397\% \text{ per day.}$$

INPUTS	273		-100	0	
	(N)	(I/YR)	(PV)	(PMT)	(FV)
OUTPUT					-107.77

Enter I in one step.
Leave data in calculator.

Now suppose you leave your money in the bank for 21 months, which is 1.75 years or 273 + 365 = 638 days.

How much will be in your account on October 1, 1995?

ANS. Override N = 273 with n = 638. FV = **$119.10.**

i_{Per} = 0.027397% per day.

```
0            365           638
├┼┼┼┼┼○○○┼┼┼├┼┼┼┼┼┼○○○○┼┼┼┤
-100                    FV = 119.10
```

$$FV = \$100(1 + 0.10 / 365)^{638}$$
$$= \$100(1.00027397)^{638}$$
$$= \$100(1.1910)$$
$$= \$119.10.$$

Copyright © 1996 by The Dryden Press. All rights reserved.

You are offered a bond which pays $1,000 in 15 months (or 456 days) for $850. You have $850 in a bank which pays a 7.0% nominal rate, with 365 daily compounding, which is a daily rate of 0.019178% and an EAR of 7.25%. You plan to leave the money in the bank if you don't buy the bond. The bond is riskless. Should you buy it?

$i_{Per} = 0.019178\%$ per day.

Days

0   365   456

-850   1,000

3 WAYS TO SOLVE:

1. Greatest future wealth: **FV**
2. Greatest wealth today: **PV**
3. Highest rate of return: Highest **EFF%**

1. Greatest Future Wealth:

Find FV of $850 left in bank for 15 months and compare with the bond's FV = $1,000.

$$FV_{Bank} = \$850(1.00019178)^{456}$$
$$= \$927.67 \text{ in bank.}$$

Buy the bond: $1,000 > $927.67.

Copyright © 1996 by The Dryden Press. All rights reserved.

CALCULATOR SOLUTION TO FV:

$$i_{Per} = i_{Nom}/m$$
$$= 7.0\%/365$$
$$= 0.019178\% \text{ per day.}$$

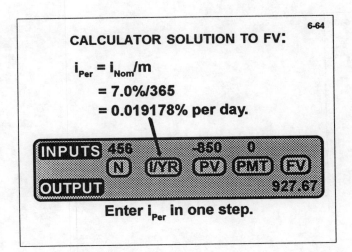

Enter i_{Per} in one step.

---

2. Greatest Present Wealth:
Find PV of bond, and compare with its $850 cost:
$$PV = \$1000/(1.00019178)^{456}$$
$$= \$916.27 .$$

```
            7/365 =
INPUTS  455 .019178        0    1000
        (N) (I/YR) (PV) (PMT) (FV)
OUTPUT              -916.27
```

PV of the bond is greater than its $850 cost, so buy bond. Raises your wealth.

BLUEPRINTS: CHAPTER 6

Copyright © 1996 by The Dryden Press. All rights reserved.

3. Rate of Return:

Find the EFF% on bond and compare with 7.25% bank pays, which is your <u>opportunity cost of capital</u>:

$$FV_n = PV(1+i)^n$$

$$\$1{,}000 = \$850(1 + i)^{456}.$$

Now must solve for i.

INPUTS 456   -850   0   1000

(N) (I/YR) (PV) (PMT) (FV)

OUTPUT 0.035646% per day

Convert % to decimal:

Decimal = 0.035646/100 = 0.00035646.

$$EAR = EFF\% = (1.00035646)^{365} - 1$$
$$= 13.89\%.$$

Using interest conversion:

P/YR = 365

NOM% = 0.035646(365) = 13.01

EFF% = 13.89

Since 13.89% > 7.25% opportunity cost, buy bond.

Copyright © 1996 by The Dryden Press. All rights reserved.

EXAM-TYPE PROBLEMS

1. Which of the following statements is most correct?

   a. The first payment under a 3-year, annual payment, amortized loan for $1,000 will include a *smaller* percentage (or fraction) of interest if the interest rate is 5% than if it is 10%.

   b. If you are lending money, then, based on effective interest rates, you should prefer to lend at a 10% nominal, or quoted, rate but with semiannual payments, rather than at a 10.1% nominal rate with annual payments. However, as a borrower you should prefer the annual payment loan.

   c. The value of a perpetuity (say for $100 per year) will approach infinity as the interest rate used to evaluate the perpetuity approaches zero.

   d. Statements a, b, and c are all true.

   e. Only statements b and c are true.

2. You want to buy a Nissan 300Z on your 27th birthday. You have priced these cars and found that they currently sell for $25,000. You believe that the price will increase by 10 percent per year until you are ready to buy. You can presently invest to earn 14 percent. If you just turned 20 years old, how much must you invest at the end of each of the next 7 years to be able to purchase the Nissan in 7 years?

3. On January 1, 1995, a graduate student developed a 5-year financial plan which would provide enough money at the end of her graduate work (January 1, 2000) to open a business of her own. Her plan was to deposit $8,000 per year for 5 years, starting immediately, into an account paying 10 percent compounded annually. Her activities proceeded according to plan except that at the end of her third year (1/1/98) she withdrew $5,000 to take a Caribbean cruise, at the end of the fourth year (1/1/99) she withdrew $5,000 to buy a used Prelude, and at the end of the fifth year (1/1/00) she had to withdraw $5,000 to pay to have her dissertation typed. Her account, at the end of the fifth year, was less than the amount she had originally planned on by how much?

4. You have just taken out a 30-year, $120,000 mortgage on your new home. This mortgage is to be repaid in 360 equal end-of-month installments. If each of the monthly installments is $1,500, what is the effective annual interest rate on this mortgage?

5. Assume that your father is now 50 years old, that he plans to retire in 10 years, and that he expects to live for 25 years after he retires, that is, until he is 85. He wants a

---

Copyright © 1996 by The Dryden Press. All rights reserved.

fixed retirement income that has the same purchasing power at the time he retires as $40,000 has today (he realizes that the real value of his retirement income will decline year-by-year after he retires). His retirement income will begin the day he retires, 10 years from today, and he will then get 24 additional annual payments. Inflation is expected to be 5 percent per year from today forward; he currently has $100,000 saved up; and he expects to earn a return on his savings of 8 percent per year, annual compounding. To the nearest dollar, how much must he save during each of the next 10 years (with deposits being made at the end of each year) to meet his retirement goal?

Copyright © 1996 by The Dryden Press. All rights reserved.

7-15 Robert Black and Carol Alvarez are vice-presidents of Western Money Management and codirectors of the company's pension fund management division. A major new client, the California League of Cities, has requested that Western present an investment seminar to the mayors of the represented cities, and Black and Alvarez, who will make the actual presentation, have asked you to help them by answering the following questions. Because the Walt Disney Company operates in one of the league's cities, you are to work Disney into the presentation. (See the vignette which opened the chapter for information on Disney.)

a. What are the key features of a bond?

b. What are call provisions and sinking fund provisions? Do these provisions make bonds more or less risky?

c. How is the value of any asset whose value is based on expected future cash flows determined?

d. How is the value of a bond determined? What is the value of a 10-year, $1,000 par value bond with a 10 percent annual coupon if its required rate of return is 10 percent?

e. (1) What would be the value of the bond described in Part d if, just after it had been issued, the expected inflation rate rose by 3 percentage points, causing investors to require a 13 percent return? Would we now have a discount or a premium bond? (If you do not have a financial calculator, $PVIF_{13\%,10} = 0.2946$; $PVIFA_{13\%,10} = 5.4262$.)

   (2) What would happen to the bonds' value if inflation fell, and k_d declined to 7 percent? Would we now have a premium or a discount bond?

   (3) What would happen to the value of the 10-year bond over time if the required rate of return remained at 13 percent, or if it remained at 7 percent? (Hint: with a financial calculator, enter PMT, I, FV, and N, and then change (override) N to see what happens to the PV as the bond approaches maturity.)

Copyright © 1996 by The Dryden Press. All rights reserved.

f. (1) What is the yield to maturity on a 10-year, 9 percent annual coupon, $1,000 par value bond that sells for $887.00? That sells for $1,134.20? What does the fact that a bond sells at a discount or at a premium tell you about the relationship between k_d and the bond's coupon rate?

   (2) What are the total return, the current yield, and the capital gains yield for the discount bond? (Assume the bond is held to maturity and the company does not default on the bonds.)

g. What is *interest rate (or price) risk*? Which bond has more interest rate risk, an annual payment 1-year bond or a 30-year bond? Why?

h. What is *reinvestment rate risk*? Which has more reinvestment rate risk, a 1-year bond or a 10-year bond?

i. How does the equation for valuing a bond change if semiannual payments are made? Find the value of a 10-year, semiannual payment, 10 percent coupon bond if nominal k_d = 13%. (Hint: $PVIF_{6.5\%,20}$ = 0.2838 and $PVIFA_{6.5\%,20}$ = 11.0185.)

j. Suppose you could buy, for $1,000, either a 10 percent, 10-year, annual payment bond or a 10 percent, 10-year, semiannual payment bond. They are equally risky. Which would you prefer? If $1,000 is the proper price for the semiannual bond, what is the equilibrium price for the annual payment bond?

k. Suppose a 10-year, 10 percent, semiannual coupon bond with a par value of $1,000 is currently selling for $1,135.90, producing a nominal yield to maturity of 8 percent. However, the bond can be called after 5 years for a price of $1,050.

   (1) What is the bond's *nominal yield to call (YTC)*?

   (2) If you bought this bond, do you think you would be more likely to earn the YTM or the YTC? Why?

l. Disney's bonds were issued with a yield to maturity of 7.5 percent. Does the yield to maturity represent the promised or expected return on the bond?

m. Disney's bonds were rated AA- by S&P. Would you consider these bonds investment grade or junk bonds?

n. What factors determine a company's bond rating?

o. If Disney were to default on the bonds, would the company be immediately liquidated? Would the bondholders be assured of receiving all of their promised payments?

Copyright © 1996 by The Dryden Press. All rights reserved.

CHAPTER 7
Bonds and Their Valuation

- Key Features of Bonds
- Bond Valuation
- Measuring Yield
- Assessing Risk

Key features of a bond:

1. **Par value:** Face amount; paid at maturity. Assume $1,000.
2. **Coupon interest rate:** Stated interest rate. Multiply by par to get $ of interest. Generally fixed.

3. **Maturity:** Years until bond must be repaid. Declines.

4. **Issue date:** Date when the bond was issued.

Copyright © 1996 by The Dryden Press. All rights reserved.

How does adding a "call provision" affect a bond?

- Issuer can refund if rates decline. That helps the issuer but hurts investors.

- Therefore, borrowers are willing to pay more, and lenders require more, on callable bonds.

- Most bonds have a deferred call and a declining call premium.

What's a "sinking fund"?

- Provision to pay off a loan over its life rather than all at maturity.

- Similar to amortization on a term loan.

- Reduces risk to investor, shortens average maturity.

- But not good for investors if rates decline after issuance.

Sinking funds are generally handled in 2 ways:

1) Call x% at par per year for S.F. purposes.

2) Buy bonds on open market.

Company would call if k_d is below the coupon rate and bond sells at a premium, use open market purchase if k_d is above coupon rate and bond sells at a discount.

Copyright © 1996 by The Dryden Press. All rights reserved.

Financial asset values:

$$0 \quad k \quad 1 \quad 2 \quad n$$

Value CF_1 CF_2 CF_n

$$PV = \frac{CF_1}{(1+k)^1} + \frac{CF_2}{(1+k)^2} + ... + \frac{CF_n}{(1+k)^n}.$$

- **The discount rate (k_I) is the <u>opportunity cost of capital</u>, i.e., the rate that could be earned on alternative investments of equal risk.**

$$k_i = k^* + IP + LP + MRP + DRP.$$

What's the value of a 10-year, 10% coupon bond if $k_d = 10\%$?

$$0 \quad 10\% \quad 1 \quad 2 \quad 10$$

V = ?   100   100   100+1000

$$V_B = \frac{\$100}{(1+k_d)^1} + \cdots + \frac{\$100}{(1+k_d)^{10}} + \frac{\$1,000}{(1+k_d)^{10}}$$
$$= \$90.91 + \cdots + \$38.55 + \$385.54$$
$$= \$1,000.$$

BLUEPRINTS: CHAPTER 7

Copyright © 1996 by The Dryden Press. All rights reserved.

The bond consists of a 10-yr, 10% annuity of $100/yr plus a $1,000 lump sum at t = 10:

PV annuity   = $ 614.46
PV maturity value = 385.54
PV annuity   = $1000.00

INPUTS	10	10		100	1,000
	N	I/YR	PV	PMT	FV
OUTPUT			-1,000		

What would happen if expected inflation rose by 3%, causing k = 13%?

INPUTS	10	13		100	1,000
	N	I/YR	PV	PMT	FV
OUTPUT			-837.21		

When k_d rises <u>above</u> the coupon rate, the bond's value falls <u>below par</u>, so it sells at a <u>discount</u>.

What would happen if inflation fell, and k_d declined to 7%?

INPUTS	10	7		100	1,000
	N	I/YR	PV	PMT	FV
OUTPUT			-1,210.71		

Price rises above par, and bond sells at a premium, if Coupon > k_d.

BLUEPRINTS: CHAPTER 7

Copyright © 1996 by The Dryden Press. All rights reserved.

The bond was issued 20 years ago and now has 10 years to maturity. What would happen to its value over time if the required rate of return remained at 10%, or at 13%, or at 7%?

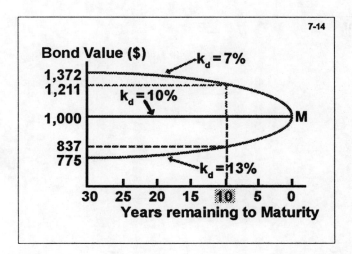

Bond Value ($)

$k_d = 7\%$
1,372
1,211
$k_d = 10\%$
1,000 ──────────────── M
837
775
$k_d = 13\%$

30   25   20   15   10   5   0
Years remaining to Maturity

- At maturity, the value of any bond must equal its par value.
- The value of a premium bond would decrease to $1,000.
- The value of a discount bond would increase to $1,000.
- A par bond stays at $1,000 if k_d remains constant.

Copyright © 1996 by The Dryden Press. All rights reserved.

What's "yield to maturity"?

- **YTM** is the rate of return earned on a bond held to maturity. Also called "promised yield".

What's the YTM on a 10-year, 9% annual coupon, $1,000 par value bond that sells for $887?

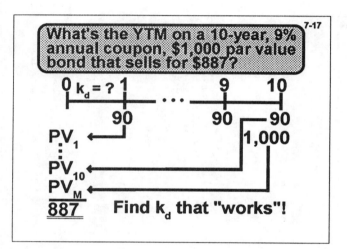

Find k_d that "works"!

Find k_d:

$$V_B = \frac{INT}{(1+k_d)^1} + \cdots + \frac{INT}{(1+k_d)^N} + \frac{M}{(1+k_d)^N}.$$

$$887 = \frac{90}{(1+k_d)^1} + \cdots + \frac{90}{(1+k_d)^{10}} + \frac{1,000}{(1+k_d)^{10}}.$$

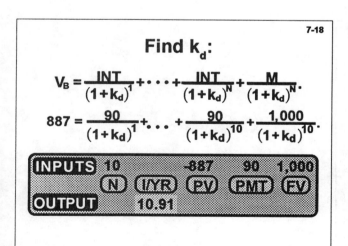

INPUTS	10		-887	90	1,000
	(N)	(I/YR)	(PV)	(PMT)	(FV)
OUTPUT		10.91			

Copyright © 1996 by The Dryden Press. All rights reserved.

- If coupon rate > k_d, premium.
- If coupon rate < k_d, discount.
- If coupon rate = k_d, par bond.
- If k_d rises, price falls.
- Price = Par at maturity.

Find YTM if price were $1,134.20

INPUTS	10		-1,134.2	90	1,000
	(N)	(I/YR)	(PV)	(PMT)	(FV)
OUTPUT		7.08			

Sells at a premium. Because coupon = 9% > k_d = 7.08%, bond's value > par.

Definitions:

$$\text{Current yield} = \frac{\text{Annual coupon pmt}}{\text{Current price}}$$

$$\text{Cap gains yld} = \frac{\text{Change in price}}{\text{Beginning price}}$$

$$\text{Exp total return} = \text{YTM} = \frac{\text{Exp}}{\text{Curr yld}} + \frac{\text{Exp cap}}{\text{gains yld}}$$

Copyright © 1996 by The Dryden Press. All rights reserved.

Find current yield and capital gains yield for a 9%, 10-year bond when the bond sells for $887 and YTM = 10.91%.

Current yield = $\dfrac{\$90}{\$887}$

$\qquad\qquad = 0.1015 = \boxed{10.15\%.}$

YTM = Curr. yld. + Cap. gains yld.

Cap. gains yld. = YTM - Curr. yld.
$\qquad\qquad\quad$ = 10.91% - 10.15%
$\qquad\qquad\quad$ = $\boxed{0.76\%.}$

Could also find value in Years 1 and 2, get difference, and divide by value in Year 1. Same answer.

What's interest rate (or price) risk? Does a 1-yr or 10-yr 10% bond have more risk?

Interest rate risk: Rising k_d causes bond's price to fall.

k_d	1-year	Change	10-Year	Change
5%	$1,048		$1,386	
		4.8%		38.6%
10%	1,000		1,000	
		4.4%		25.1%
15%	956		749	

Copyright © 1996 by The Dryden Press. All rights reserved.

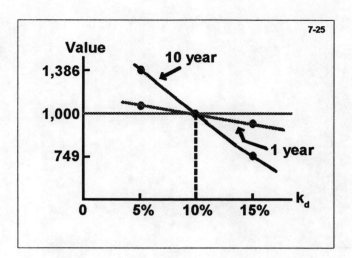

7-25

7-26

⟨What is reinvestment rate risk?⟩

The risk that CFs will have to be reinvested in the future at lower rates, reducing income.

Illustration: **Suppose you just won $500,000 playing the lottery. You'll invest the money and live off the interest. You buy a 1-year bond with a YTM of 10%.**

7-27

Year 1 income = $50,000. At year-end get back $500,000 to reinvest.

If rates fall to 3%, income will drop from $50,000 to $15,000. Had you bought 30-year bonds, income would have remained constant.

Copyright © 1996 by The Dryden Press. All rights reserved.

- **Long-term bonds:** High interest rate risk, low reinvestment rate risk.

- **Short-term bonds:** Low interest rate risk, high reinvestment rate risk.

- **Nothing is riskless!**

True or False: "All 10-year bonds have the same price and reinvestment rate risk."

False! Low coupon bonds have less reinvestment rate but more price risk than high coupon bonds.

Semi-annual Bonds

1. Multiply years by 2 to get periods = 2n.
2. Divide nominal rate by 2 to get periodic rate = k/2
3. Divide annual INT by 2 to get PMT = INT/2.

INPUTS 2n k/2 OK INT/2 OK
         N I/YR PV PMT FV
OUTPUT

Copyright © 1996 by The Dryden Press. All rights reserved.

Find value of 10-year, 10% coupon, semiannual bond if $k_d = 13\%$.

	2(10)	13/2		100/2	
INPUTS	20	6.5		50	1,000
	(N)	(I/YR)	(PV)	(PMT)	(FV)
OUTPUT			-834.72		

You could buy, for $1,000, either a 10%, 10-year, annual payment bond or an equally risky 10%, 10-year, semiannual bond. Which would you prefer?

The semiannual bond's EFF% is:

$$EFF\% = \left(1 + \frac{i_{Nom}}{m}\right)^m - 1 = \left(1 + \frac{0.10}{2}\right)^2 - 1 = 10.25\%.$$

10.25% > 10% EFF% on annual bond, so buy semiannual bond.

If $1,000 is the proper price for the semiannual bond, what is the proper price for the annual payment bond?

- **Semiannual bond has $k_{Nom} = 10\%$, with EFF% = 10.25%. Should earn same EFF% on annual payment bond, so:**

INPUTS	10	10.25		100	1,000
	(N)	(I/YR)	(PV)	(PMT)	(FV)
OUTPUT			-984.80		

BLUEPRINTS: CHAPTER 7

Copyright © 1996 by The Dryden Press. All rights reserved.

- At a price of $984.80, the annual and semiannual bonds would be in equilibrium, because investors would earn EFF% = 10.25% on either bond.

A 10-year, 10% semiannual coupon, $1,000 par value bond is selling for $1,135.90 with an 8% yield to maturity. It can be called after 5 years at $1,050.

What's the bond's nominal yield to call (YTC)?

INPUTS	10		-1,135.9	50	1,050
	(N)	(I/YR)	(PV)	(PMT)	(FV)
OUTPUT		$3.765 \times 2 = 7.53\%$			

k_{NOM} = 7.53% is the rate brokers would quote. Could also calculate EFF% to call:

$$EFF\% = (1.03765)^2 - 1 = 7.672\%.$$

This rate could be compared to monthly mortgages, etc.

Copyright © 1996 by The Dryden Press. All rights reserved.

If you bought bond, would you be more likely to earn YTM or YTC?

- Coupon rate = 10% vs. YTC = k_d = 7.53%. Could raise money by selling new bonds which pay 7.53%.
- Could thus replace bonds which pay $100/year with bonds that pay only $75.30/year.
- Investors should expect a call, hence YTC = 7.5%, not YTM = 8%.

- In general, if a bond sells at a premium, then (1) coupon > k_d, so (2) a call is likely.

- So, expect to earn:

  YTC on premium bonds.

  YTM on par & discount bonds.

Default risk

- If issuer defaults, investors receive less than the promised return. Therefore, the expected return on corporate and municipal bonds is less than the promised return.
- Disney recently issued 100-year bonds with a YTM of 7.5%--this represents the promised return. The expected return was less than 7.5% when the bonds were issued.

Copyright © 1996 by The Dryden Press. All rights reserved.

Bond Ratings Provide One Measure of Default Risk

MOODY'S AND S&P BOND RATINGS

	Investment Grade				Junk Bonds			
Moody's	Aaa	Aa	A	Baa	Ba	B	Caa	C
S&P	AAA	AA	A	BBB	BB	B	CCC	D

What factors affect default risk and bond ratings?

- **Financial performance**
  - Debt Ratio
  - TIE, FCC ratios
  - Current ratio

- **Provisions in the bond contract**
  - Secured vs. unsecured debt
  - Senior vs. subordinated debt
  - Guarantee provisions
  - Sinking fund provisions
  - Debt maturity

Copyright © 1996 by The Dryden Press. All rights reserved.

■ **Other factors**
  · **Earnings potential**
  · **Regulatory environment**
  · **Potential product liability**
  · **Accounting policies**

Bankruptcy

■ **Two main chapters of Federal Bankruptcy Act:**

  Chapter 11, Reorganization

  Chapter 7, Liquidation

■ **Typically, company wants Chapter 11, creditors may prefer Chapter 7.**

■ **If company can't meet its obliga-tions, it files under Chapter 11. That stops creditors from foreclosing, taking assets, and shutting down the business.**

Company has 120 days to file a reorganization plan.

Court appoints a "trustee" to supervise reorganization. Manage-ment usually stays in control.

Copyright © 1996 by The Dryden Press. All rights reserved.

7-46

- Company must demonstrate in its reorganization plan that it is "worth more alive than dead".

Otherwise, judge will order liquidation under Chapter 7.

7-47

- If the company is liquidated, here's the payment priority:
  1. Secured creditors from sale of securing assets
  2. Trustee's costs
  3. Wages subject to limits
  4. Taxes
  5. Unfunded pension liabilities
  6. Unsecured creditors
  7. Preferred stock
  8. Common stock

7-48

- In a liquidation, unsecured creditors generally get zero. This makes them more willing to participate in reorganization even though their claims are greatly scaled back.
- Various groups of creditors vote on the reorganization plan. If both the majority of the creditors and the judge approve, company "emerges" from bankruptcy with lower debts, reduced interest charges, and a chance for success.

Copyright © 1996 by The Dryden Press. All rights reserved.

EXAM-TYPE PROBLEMS

1. Gator Services Unlimited (GSU) needs to raise $25 million in new debt capital. GSU's currently outstanding bonds have a $1,000 par value, an 8% coupon rate, pay interest semiannually, and have 30 years remaining to maturity. The bonds are callable after 5 years at a price of $1,080, and currently sell at a price of $676.77. Right now, the yield curve is flat and is expected to remain flat for a while. The risk on GSU's new bonds is the same as for its old bonds. Based on these data, what is the best estimate of GSU's nominal interest rate on new bonds?

2. Florida Financial Corporation (FFC) purchases packages of guaranteed student loans from banks for its portfolio. FFC is considering a package with the following characteristics. The securities, which are similar to bonds, have a $1,000 par value, pay 8% interest semiannually for 5 years and then pay a stepped-up interest rate of 10% semiannually for the next 7 years. The maturity value is $1,000, paid at the end of 12 years. FFC's alternative to this investment are 9% coupon bonds, selling at par of $1,000, which pay interest quarterly. Assuming that the investments are of similar risk, how much should FFC be willing to pay for the student loan package?

3. Trickle Corporation's 12% coupon rate, semiannual payment, $1,000 par value bonds which mature in 25 years, are callable at a price of $1,080 five years from now. The bonds currently sell for $1,230.51 in the market, and the yield curve is flat. Assuming that the yield curve is expected to remain flat, what is Trickle's most likely *before-tax cost* of debt if it issues new bonds today?

4. Recycler Battery Corporation (RBC) issued zero coupon bonds 5 years ago at a price of $214.50 per bond. RBC's zeros had a 20-year original maturity, and a $1,000 par value. The bonds were callable 10 years after the issue date at a price 7% over their accrued value on the call date. If the bonds sell for $239.39 in the market today, what annual rate of return should an investor who buys the bonds today expect to earn on them? (Hint: Material covered in Appendix 7A.)

5. Suppose a new company decides to raise its initial $200 million of capital as $100 million of common equity and $100 million of long-term debt. By an iron-clad provision in its charter, the company can never borrow any more money. Which of the following statements is most correct?

   a. If the debt were raised by issuing $50 million of debentures and $50 million of first mortgage bonds, we could be absolutely certain that the firm's total interest

Copyright © 1996 by The Dryden Press. All rights reserved.

expense would be lower than if the debt were raised by issuing $100 million of debentures.

b. If the debt were raised by issuing $50 million of debentures and $50 million of first mortgage bonds, we could be absolutely certain that the firm's total interest expense would be lower than if the debt were raised by issuing $100 million of first mortgage bonds.

c. The higher the percentage of total debt represented by debentures, the greater the risk of, and hence the interest rate on, the debentures.

d. The higher the percentage of total debt represented by mortgage bonds, the riskier both types of bonds will be, and, consequently, the higher the firms' total dollar interest charges will be.

e. In this situation, we cannot tell for sure how, or whether, the firm's total interest expense on the $100 million of debt would be affected by the mix of debentures versus first mortgage bonds. Interest rates on the two types of bonds would vary as their percentages were changed, but the result might well be such that the firm's total interest charges would not be affected materially by the mix between the two.

6. Which of the following statements is most correct?

a. Because bonds can generally be called only at a premium, meaning that the bondholder will enjoy a capital gain, including a call provision (other than a sinking fund call) in the indenture increases the value of the bond and lowers the bond's required rate of return.

b. You are considering two bonds. Both are rated AA, both mature in 20 years, both have a 10 percent coupon, and both are offered to you at their $1,000 par value. However, Bond X has a sinking fund while Bond Y does not. This is probably not an equilibrium situation, as Bond X, which has the sinking fund, would generally be expected to have a higher yield than Bond Y.

c. A sinking fund provides for the orderly retirement of a debt (or preferred stock) issue. Sinking funds generally force the firm to call a percentage of the issue each year. However, the call price for sinking fund purposes is generally higher than the call price for refunding purposes.

d. Zero coupon bonds are bought primarily by pension funds and other tax exempt investors because they avoid the tax that non-tax exempt investors must pay on the accrued value each year.

e. All of the above statements are false.

Copyright © 1996 by The Dryden Press. All rights reserved.

8-18 Robert Black and Carol Alvarez are vice-presidents of Western Money Management and codirectors of the company's pension fund management division. A major new client, the California League of Cities, has requested that Western present an investment seminar on common stock valuation to the mayors of the represented cities, and Black and Alvarez, who will make the actual presentation, have asked you to help them by answering the following questions. Because the Walt Disney Company operates in one of the league's cities, you are to work Disney into the presentation.

a. Describe briefly the legal rights and privileges of common stockholders.

b. (1)   Write out and explain a formula that can be used to value any stock, regardless of its dividend pattern.

   (2)   What is a constant growth stock? How are constant growth stocks valued?

   (3)   What happens if the constant g exceeds k_s? Will many stocks have $g > k_s$ in the short run? In the long run (i.e., forever)?

c. Assume that Disney has a beta coefficient of 1.2, that the risk-free rate (the yield on T-bonds) is 6 percent, and that the required rate of return on the market is 11 percent. What is the required rate of return on Disney's stock?

d. Assume that Disney is a constant growth company whose last dividend (D_0, which was paid yesterday) was $0.25, and whose dividend is expected to grow indefinitely at a 6 percent rate.

   (1)   What would Disney's expected dividend stream be over the next 3 years, and what is the PV of each dividend?

   (2)   Under these conditions, what would be Disney's current stock price? Note that $g = 6\%$, $k_s = 12\%$.

   (3)   What should the stock's expected value be 1 year from now?

   (4)   Calculate the expected dividend yield, the capital gains yield, and the total return during the first year.

Copyright © 1996 by The Dryden Press. All rights reserved.

e. Now assume that the stock is currently selling at $4.42. What is the expected rate of return on the stock?

f. What would the stock price be if Disney's dividends were expected to have zero growth?

g. Now assume that Disney is expected to experience supernormal dividend growth of 30 percent for the next 3 years, then to fall to a long-run constant growth rate of 10 percent. What would the stock's value be under these conditions? What would its expected dividend yield and capital gains yield be in Year 1? In Year 4?

h. Suppose Disney was expected to experience zero growth during the next 3 years and then to achieve a constant growth rate of 11 percent in the fourth year and thereafter. What would be the stock's value now? What is its expected dividend yield and its capital gains yield in Year 1? In Year 4?

i. Finally, assume that Disney's earnings and dividends are expected to decline by a constant 6 percent per year, that is, $g = -6\%$. Would you or anyone else be willing to buy such a stock? At what price should it sell? What would be the dividend yield and capital gains yield in each year?

j. What does market equilibrium mean?

k. If equilibrium does not exist, how will it be established?

l. What are the various forms of market efficiency? What are the implications of market efficiency?

m. The CaliforniaLleague of Cities is also interested in preferred stock. Briefly describe some of the advantages and disadvantages of preferred stock.

n. Taylor Company recently issued preferred stock with a constant dividend of $5 per year, at a share price of $50. What is the expected return on the company's preferred stock?

Copyright © 1996 by The Dryden Press. All rights reserved.

CHAPTER 8
Stocks and Their Valuation

- Features of Common Stock
- Determining Common Stock Values
- Efficient Markets
- Preferred Stock

Facts about Common Stock:

1. Represents ownership.
2. Ownership implies control.
3. Stockholders elect directors.
4. Directors elect management.
5. Management's goal: Max. stock price.

Social/Ethical Question:

Should mgt. be equally concerned about employees, customers, suppliers, "the public", or just the stockholders?

In enterprise economy, work for stockholder subject to constraints (environmental, fair hiring, etc.) and competition.

BLUEPRINTS: CHAPTER 8

Copyright © 1996 by The Dryden Press. All rights reserved.

8-4

Advantages of Financing with Stock:

- No required fixed payments.

- No maturity.

- Improves debt ratio, coverage.

8-5

Disadvantages of Financing with Stock:

- Controlling shareholders may lose some control.

- Future earnings shared with new stockholders. Dilution.

- Higher flotation costs vs. debt.

- Higher component cost of capital.

- Too little debt may encourage a takeover bid.

8-6

What's classified stock? How might classified stock be used?

- Classified stock has special provisions.

- Could classify existing stock as founder's shares, with voting rights but dividend restrictions.

- New shares might be called "Class A" shares, with voting restrictions but full dividend rights.

Copyright © 1996 by The Dryden Press. All rights reserved.

When is a stock sale an initial public offering (IPO)?

- A firm "goes public" through an IPO when the stock is first offered to the public.

Stock Value = PV of Dividends

$$\hat{P}_0 = \frac{D_1}{(1+k_s)^1} + \frac{D_2}{(1+k_s)^2} + \frac{D_3}{(1+k_s)^3} + \cdots + \frac{D_\infty}{(1+k_s)^\infty}.$$

What is a constant growth stock?

One whose dividends are expected to grow forever at a constant rate, g.

For a constant growth stock,

$$D_1 = D_0(1+g)^1,$$
$$D_2 = D_0(1+g)^2,$$
$$D_t = D_0(1+g)^t.$$

If g is constant, then:

$$\hat{P}_0 = \frac{D_0(1+g)}{k_s - g} = \frac{D_1}{k_s - g}.$$

BLUEPRINTS: CHAPTER 8

Copyright © 1996 by The Dryden Press. All rights reserved.

$$D_t = D_0(1 + g)^t$$

$$PVD_t = \frac{D_t}{(1 + k)^t}$$

If g > k,
$$P_0 = \infty \, !$$

$$P_0 = \sum PVD_t$$

0.25

0

Years (t)

What happens if g > k_s?

$$\hat{P}_0 = \frac{D_1}{k_s - g} \text{ requires } k_s > g.$$

- If k_s < g, get negative stock price, which is nonsense.

- We can't use model unless (1) k_s > g and (2) g is expected to be constant forever. See #10.

Assume beta = 1.2 , k_{RF} = 6%, and k_M = 11%. What is the required rate of return on the firm's stock?

Use the SML to calculate k_s:

$$k_s = k_{RF} + (k_M - k_{RF})b_{Firm}$$
$$= 6\% + (11\% - 6\%)(1.2)$$
$$= 12\%.$$

BLUEPRINTS: CHAPTER 8

Copyright © 1996 by The Dryden Press. All rights reserved.

D_0 was $0.25 and g is a constant 6%. Find the expected dividends for the next 3 years, and their PVs. $k_s = 12\%$.

| 0 | | 1 | 2 | 3 | 4 |

g = 6%

$D_0 = 0.25$ 0.265   0.2809   0.2978

12%

0.2366
0.2239
0.2120

What's the stock's market value? $D_0 = 0.25$, k = 12%, g = 6%.

Constant growth model:

$$\hat{P}_0 = \frac{D_1}{k_s - g} = \frac{\$0.265}{0.12 - 0.06}$$

$$= \frac{\$0.265}{0.06} = \$4.42.$$

What is the stock's expected value one year from now, $\hat{P}_1$?

- D_1 will have been paid, so expected dividends are D_2, D_3, D_4, and so on. Thus,

$$\hat{P}_1 = \frac{D_2}{k_s - g} = \frac{\$0.2809}{0.12 - 0.06}$$

$$= \$4.68.$$

- Could also find P_1 as follows:

$$P_1 = P_0(1 + g) = \$4.42(1.06) = \$4.68.$$

BLUEPRINTS: CHAPTER 8

Copyright © 1996 by The Dryden Press. All rights reserved.

Find the expected dividend yield, capital gains yield, and total return during the first year.

$$\text{Dividend yield} = \frac{D_1}{P_0} = \frac{\$0.265}{\$4.42} = 6\%.$$

$$\text{Capital gains yield} = \frac{\hat{P}_1 - P_0}{P_0} = k - \frac{D_1}{P_0} = 6\%.$$

$$\text{Total Return} = 6\% + 6\% = 12\%.$$

Rearrange model to rate of return form:

$$P_0 = \frac{D_1}{k_s - g} \text{ to } \hat{k}_s = \frac{D_1}{P_0} + g.$$

$$\text{Then, } \hat{k}_s = \$0.265/\$4.42 + 0.06$$
$$= 0.06 + 0.06 = 12\%.$$

What would P_0 be if g = 0?

The dividend stream would be a perpetuity.

```
0    12%   1         2         3
|----------|---------|---------|----••••>
          0.25      0.25      0.25
```

$$P_0 = \frac{PMT}{k} = \frac{\$0.25}{0.12} = \$2.08.$$

Copyright © 1996 by The Dryden Press. All rights reserved.

If we have supernormal growth of 30% for 3 yrs, then a long-run constant g = 10%, what is $\hat{P}_0$? k is still 12%.

- Can no longer use constant growth model.

- However, growth becomes constant after 3 years.

Nonconstant growth followed by constant growth:

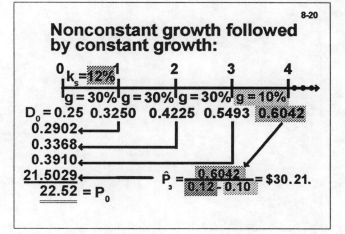

$$\hat{P}_3 = \frac{0.6042}{0.12 - 0.10} = \$30.21.$$

What is the expected dividend yield and capital gains yield at t = 0? At t = 4?

$$\text{Div. yield}_0 = \frac{\$0.3250}{\$22.52} = 1.44\%$$

$$\text{Cap. gain}_0 = 12\% - 1.44\% = 10.56\%$$

BLUEPRINTS: CHAPTER 8

Copyright © 1996 by The Dryden Press. All rights reserved.

- During nonconstant growth, D/P and cap. gains yield not constant, and capital gains yield is less than g.

- After t = 3, g = constant = 10% = capital gains yield; k = 12%; so D/P = 12 - 10 = 2%.

Suppose g = 0 for t = 1 to 3, and then g is a constant 11%. What is $\hat{P}_0$?

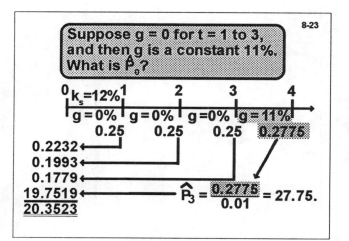

$$\hat{P}_3 = \frac{0.2775}{0.01} = 27.75.$$

What is D/P and capital gains yield at t = 0 and at t = 3?

$t = 0:$ $\dfrac{D_1}{P_0} = \dfrac{\$0.25}{\$20.35} = 1.23\%.$

$CGY = 12\% - 1.23\% = 10.77\%.$

$t = 3:$ Now have constant growth with g = cap. gains yield = 11% and D/P = 1%.

Copyright © 1996 by The Dryden Press. All rights reserved.

If g = -6%, would anyone buy the stock? If so, at what price?

Firm still has earnings and still pays dividends, so $P_0 > 0$:

$$\hat{P}_0 = \frac{D_1}{k_s - g} = \frac{D_0(1+g)}{k_s - g}$$

$$= \frac{\$0.25(0.94)}{0.12 - (-0.06)} = \frac{\$0.235}{0.18} = \$1.31.$$

What is the annual D/P and capital gains yield?

Capital gains yield = g = -6.0%,

Dividend yield = 12.0% - (-6.0%) = 18%.

D/P and cap. gains yield are constant, with high dividend yield (18%) offsetting negative cap. gains yield.

What is market equilibrium?

In equilibrium, stock prices are stable. There is no general tendency for people to buy versus sell.

In equilibrium, expected returns must equal required returns:

$$\hat{k} = D_1 / P_0 + g = k = k_{RF} + (k_M - k_{RF})b.$$

Copyright © 1996 by The Dryden Press. All rights reserved.

How is equilibrium established?

8-28

If $\hat{k} = \dfrac{D_1}{P_0} + g > k$, then

P_0 is "too low", a bargain.

Buy orders > Sell orders; P_0 bid up; D_1/P_0 falls until $D_1/P_0 + g = \hat{k} = k$.

Why do stock prices change?

8-29

$$P_0 = \frac{D_1}{k_i - g}$$

1. k_i could change:
$k_i = k_{RF} + (k_M - k_{RF})b_i$
$k_{RF} = k^* + IP$

2. g could change due to economic or firm situation.

8-30

Feb. 4, 1994: Fed announced increase in interest rates at 11 a.m.

Result: Dow Jones fell 95 points.

BLUEPRINTS: CHAPTER 8

Copyright © 1996 by The Dryden Press. All rights reserved.

What's the Efficient Markets Hypothesis?

EMH: Securities are normally in equilibrium and are "fairly priced." One cannot "beat the market" except through good luck or inside info.

1. Weak-form EMH:

Can't profit by looking at past trends. A recent decline is no reason to think stocks will go up (or down) in the future. Seems empirically true, but "technical analysis" is still used.

2. Semistrong-form efficiency:

All publicly available info. is reflected in stock prices, so doesn't pay to pore over annual reports looking for undervalued stocks. Largely true, but superior analysts can still profit by finding and using new information.

Copyright © 1996 by The Dryden Press. All rights reserved.

3. **Strong-form efficiency:**
   All information, even inside info, is embedded in stock prices. Not true--insiders can gain by trading on the basis of insider information, but that's illegal.

Markets are efficient because:

1. 15,000 or so trained analysts; MBAs, CFAs, Technical PhDs.

2. Work for firms like Merrill, Morgan, Prudential, which have much money.

3. Have similar access to data.

4. Thus, news is reflected in P_0 almost instantaneously.

Preferred Stock

- Hybrid security.
- Similar to bonds in that preferred stockholders receive a fixed dividend which must be paid before dividends can be paid on common stock.
- However, unlike interest payments on bonds companies can omit dividend payments on preferred stock without fear of pushing the firm into bankruptcy.

BLUEPRINTS: CHAPTER 8

Copyright © 1996 by The Dryden Press. All rights reserved.

Major Provisions of Preferred Stock

- Preferred stockholders have priority over common stockholders.
- Par value of preferred stock is meaningful and affects what preferred stockholders receive in bankruptcy.
- Most preferred stock provides for cumulative dividends.
- Many issues can be converted to common stock.

Advantages and Disadvantages of Preferred Stock: The Issuer's Perspective

- Preferred stock (unless it is participating) has a fixed dividend which enables an issuer to fix its costs and therefore keep more of its profits for common stockholders.
- By selling preferred stock rather than common the firm avoids sharing control with new investors.
- Major disadvantage is that preferred stock payments are not deductible which makes preferred stock more costly than debt.

Advantages of Preferred Stock: The Investor's Perspective

- Provides steadier and more reliable income than common stock.
- Higher priority than common stock in the event of liquidation.
- 70% of preferred dividends received by corporations are not taxable. For this reason most preferred stock is owned by corporations.

Copyright © 1996 by The Dryden Press. All rights reserved.

Disadvantages of Preferred Stock: The Investor's Perspective

- However, unlike common stock the returns on preferred stock are limited.
- For individuals after-tax bond yields are often higher than the after-tax yields on preferred stock, even though preferred stock is riskier.

What's the expected return of preferred stock with P = $50 and annual dividend = $5?

$$P = \$50 = \frac{\$5}{\hat{k}_{ps}}$$

$$\hat{k}_{ps} = \frac{\$5}{\$50} = 0.10 = 10.0\%.$$

Copyright © 1996 by The Dryden Press. All rights reserved.

EXAM-TYPE PROBLEMS

1. Carlson Products, a constant growth company, has a current market (and equilibrium) stock price of $20.00. Carlson's next dividend, D_1, is forecasted to be $2.00, and Carlson is growing at an annual rate of 6 percent. Carlson has a beta coefficient of 1.2, and the required rate of return on the market is 15 percent. As Carlson's financial manager, you have access to insider information concerning a switch in product lines which would not change the growth rate, but would cut Carlson's beta coefficient in half. If you buy the stock at the current market price, what is your expected percentage capital gain?

2. The Hart Mountain Company has recently discovered a new type of kitty litter which is extremely absorbent. It is expected that the firm will experience (beginning now) an unusually high growth rate (20 percent) during the period (3 years) it has exclusive rights to the property where the raw material used to make this kitty litter is found. However, beginning with the fourth year the firm's competition will have access to the material, and from that time on the firm will achieve a normal growth rate of 8 percent annually. During the rapid growth period, the firm's dividend payout ratio will be relatively low (20 percent) in order to conserve funds for reinvestment. However, the decrease in growth in the fourth year will be accompanied by an increase in dividend payout to 50 percent. Last year's earnings were $E_0 = 2.00 per share, and the firm's required return is 10 percent. What should be the current price of the common stock?

3. Which of the following statements is most correct?

   a. One of the advantages of common stock financing is that there is no dilution of owner's equity, as there is with debt.

   b. If the market price of a stock falls below its book value, the firm can be liquidated, with the book value proceeds then distributed to the shareholders. Thus, a stock's book value per share sets a floor below which the stock's market price is unlikely to fall.

   c. The preemptive right gives a firm's preferred stockholders preference to assets over common stockholders in the event the firm is liquidated.

   d. All of the above statements are true.

   e. All of the above statements are false.

Copyright © 1996 by The Dryden Press. All rights reserved.

9-17 During the last few years, Coleman Technologies has been too constrained by the high cost of capital to make many capital investments. Recently, though, capital costs have been declining, and the company has decided to look seriously at a major expansion program that had been proposed by the marketing department. Assume that you are an assistant to Jerry Lehman, the financial vice-president. Your first task is to estimate Coleman's cost of capital. Lehman has provided you with the following data, which he believes may be relevant to your task:

1. The firm's tax rate is 40 percent.

2. The current price of Coleman's 12 percent coupon, semiannual payment, noncallable bonds with 15 years remaining to maturity is $1,153.72. Coleman does not use short-term interest-bearing debt on a permanent basis. New bonds would be privately placed with no flotation cost.

3. The current price of the firm's 10 percent, $100 par value, quarterly dividend, perpetual preferred stock is $113.10. Coleman would incur flotation costs of $2.00 per share on a new issue.

4. Coleman's common stock is currently selling at $50 per share. Its last dividend (D_0) was $4.19, and dividends are expected to grow at a constant rate of 5 percent in the foreseeable future. Coleman's beta is 1.2; the yield on T-bonds is 7 percent; and the market risk premium is estimated to be 6 percent. For the bond-yield-plus-risk-premium approach, the firm uses a 4 percentage point risk premium.

5. New common stock can be sold at a flotation cost of 15 percent.

6. Coleman's target capital structure is 30 percent long-term debt, 10 percent preferred stock, and 60 percent common equity.

7. The firm is forecasting retained earnings of $300,000 for the coming year.

To structure the task somewhat, Lehman has asked you to answer the following questions.

a. (1) What sources of capital should be included when you estimate Coleman's weighted average cost of capital (WACC)?

(2) Should the component costs be figured on a before-tax or an after-tax basis?

(3) Should the costs be historical (embedded) costs or new (marginal) costs?

b. What is the market interest rate on Coleman's debt and its component cost of debt?

c. (1) What is the firm's cost of preferred stock?

(2) Coleman's preferred stock is riskier to investors than its debt, yet the preferred's yield to investors is lower than the yield to maturity on the debt. Does this suggest that you have made a mistake? (Hint: Think about taxes.)

d. (1) Why is there a cost associated with retained earnings?

(2) What is Coleman's estimated cost of retained earnings using the CAPM approach?

(3) Why is the T-bond rate a better estimate of the risk-free rate for cost of capital purposes than the T-bill rate?

e. What is the estimated cost of retained earnings using the discounted cash flow (DCF) approach?

f. What is the bond-yield-plus-risk-premium estimate for Coleman's cost of retained earnings?

g. What is your final estimate for k_s?

h. What is Coleman's cost for newly issued common stock, k_e?

i. Explain in words why new common stock has a higher percentage cost than retained earnings.

j. (1) What is Coleman's overall, or weighted average, cost of capital (WACC) when retained earnings are used as the equity component?

(2) What is the WACC after retained earnings have been exhausted and Coleman uses new common stock with a 15 percent flotation cost?

k. (1) At what amount of new investment would Coleman be forced to issue new common stock? Put another way, what is the largest capital budget the company could support without issuing new common stock? Assume that the 30/10/60 target capital structure will be maintained.

Copyright © 1996 by The Dryden Press. All rights reserved.

(2)   What is a marginal cost of capital (MCC) schedule? Construct a graph which shows Coleman's MCC schedule.

I. Coleman's director of capital budgeting has identified the three following potential projects:

Project	Cost	Rate of Return
A	$700,000	17.0%
B	500,000	15.0
C	800,000	11.5

All of the projects are equally risky, and they are all similar in risk to the company's existing assets.

(1)   Plot the IOS schedule on the same graph that contains your MCC schedule. What is the firm's marginal cost of capital for capital budgeting purposes?

(2)   What is the dollar size, and the included projects, in Coleman's optimal capital budget? Explain your answer fully.

(3)   Would Coleman's MCC schedule remain constant at 12.1 percent beyond $2 million regardless of the amount of capital required?

Copyright © 1996 by The Dryden Press. All rights reserved.

CHAPTER 9
The Cost of Capital

- Cost of Capital Components
    Debt
    Preferred
    Common Equity
- WACC
- MCC
- IOS

What types of long-term capital do firms use?

Long-term debt

Preferred stock

Common equity:

   Retained earnings
   New common stock

Should we focus on before-tax or after-tax capital costs?

Stockholders focus on A-T CFs. Thus, focus on A-T capital costs, i.e., use A-T costs in WACC. Only k_d needs adjustment.

Copyright © 1996 by The Dryden Press. All rights reserved.

Should we focus on historical (embedded) costs or new (marginal) costs?

The cost of capital is used primarily to make decisions which involve raising new capital. So, focus on today's marginal costs (for WACC).

What's k_d? Coupon = 12% semi; Price = $1,153.72; 15 years.

INPUTS	30		-1,153.72	60	1,000
	(N)	(I/YR)	(PV)	(PMT)	(FV)
OUTPUT		5.0% x 2 = k_d = 10%.			

Component cost of debt:

- Interest is **tax deductible**, so

$$k_{d\,AT} = k_{d\,BT}(1-T)$$
$$= 10\%(1-0.40) = 6\%.$$

- Use **nominal** rate.
- Flotation costs small. **Ignore.**

Copyright © 1996 by The Dryden Press. All rights reserved.

What's the cost of preferred stock? $P_p = \$113.10$; 10%Q; Par = $100; F = $2.

Use this formula:

$$k_{ps} = \frac{D_{ps}}{P_{Net}} = \frac{0.1(\$100)}{\$113.10 - \$2.00}$$

$$= \frac{\$10}{\$111.10} = 0.090 = 9.0\%.$$

Picture of Preferred:

$$0 \quad k_{ps} = ? \quad 1 \qquad 2 \qquad \infty$$

$$-111.1 \qquad 2.50 \qquad 2.50$$

$$111.10 = \frac{D}{k - g} = \frac{2.50}{k_{Per}}.$$

$$k_{Per} = \frac{2.50}{111.10} = 2.25; \quad k_{ps(Nom)} = 2.25(4) = 9\%.$$

Note:

- Flotation costs for pfd. are significant, so are reflected. Use net price.

- Pfd. dividends are not deductible, so no tax adjustment. Just k_{ps}.

- Nominal k_{ps} is used.

Copyright © 1996 by The Dryden Press. All rights reserved.

Is pfd. stock more or less risky to investors than debt?

- **More risky**: company not required to pay pfd. div.

- However, firms **try** to pay pfd. div. Otherwise, (1) cannot pay common div., (2) difficult to raise add'l funds, (3) pfd. stockholders may gain control of firm.

Why is yield on pfd. lower than k_d?

- Corporations own most preferred stock, because **70% of pfd. div. are nontaxable** to corporations.

- Therefore, pfd. often has a lower B-T yield than the B-T yield on debt.

- The **A-T yield** to an investor, and the A-T cost to the issuer, are **higher** on pfd. than on debt. Consistent with higher risk of pfd.

Example:

$k_{Pfd} = 8.84\%$ $k_d = 10\%$ $T = 40\%$

$k_{Pfd, AT} = k_{ps} - k_{ps}(1 - 0.7)(T)$

$\qquad\qquad = 8.84\% - 8.84\%(0.3)(0.4)$

$\qquad\qquad\qquad\qquad = 7.78\%$

$k_{d, AT} = 10\% - 10\%(0.4) = 6.00\%.$

A-T Risk Prem. on Pfd. = <u>1.78%</u>.

Copyright © 1996 by The Dryden Press. All rights reserved.

Why is there a cost for retained earnings?

- Earnings can be reinvested or paid out as dividends.

- Investors could buy other securities, earn a return.

- Thus, there is an opportunity cost if earnings are retained.

- Opportunity cost: The return stockholders could earn on alternative investments of equal risk.

- They could buy similar stocks and earn k_s, or company could repurchase its own stock and earn k_s. So, k_s is the cost of RE.

Three ways to determine cost of retained earnings, k_s:

1. CAPM: $k_s = k_{RF} + (k_M - k_{RF})b$.

2. DCF: $k_s = D_1/P_0 + g$.

3. Own-Bond-Yield-Plus-Risk Premium:
$$k_s = k_d + RP.$$

Copyright © 1996 by The Dryden Press. All rights reserved.

What's the cost of retained earnings based on the CAPM?
k_{RF} = 7%, MRP = 6%, b = 1.2 .

$$k_s = k_{RF} + (k_M - k_{RF})b$$

$$= 7.0\% + (6.0\%)1.2 = \boxed{14.2\%}.$$

What's the DCF cost of retained earnings, k_s? Given:
D_0 = \$4.19; P_0 = \$50; g = 5%.

$$k_s = \frac{D_1}{P_0} + g = \frac{D_0(1+g)}{P_0} + g$$

$$= \frac{\$4.19(1.05)}{\$50} + 0.05$$

$$= 0.088 + 0.05 = \boxed{13.8\%.}$$

Suppose the company has been earning 15% on equity (ROE = 15%) and retaining 35% (dividend payout = 65%), and this situation is expected to continue.

What's the expected future g?

Copyright © 1996 by The Dryden Press. All rights reserved.

Retention growth rate:

$g = b(ROE) = 0.35(15\%) = 5.25\%.$

Here b = Fraction retained.

Close to g = 5% given earlier. Think of bank account paying 10% with b = 0, b = 1.0, and b = 0.5. What's g?

Could DCF methodology be applied if g is not constant?

- **Yes, nonconstant g stocks are expected to have constant g at some point, generally in 5 to 10 years.**

- **But calculations get complicated.**

Find k_s using the own-bond-yield-plus-risk-premium method. ($k_d = 10\%$, RP = 4%.)

$k_s = k_d + RP$
$= 10.0\% + 4.0\% = 14.0\%.$

- **This RP $\neq$ CAPM RP.**
- **Produces ballpark estimate of k_s. Useful check.**

Copyright © 1996 by The Dryden Press. All rights reserved.

What's a reasonable final estimate of k_s?

Method	Estimate
CAPM	14.2%
DCF	13.8%
k_d + RP	14.0%
Average	14.0%

How do we find the cost of new common stock, k_e?

Use DCF formula, but adjust P_0 for flotation cost. End up with $k_e > k_s$.

New common, F = 15%:

$$k_e = \frac{D_0(1+g)}{P_0(1-F)} + g$$

$$= \frac{\$4.19(1.05)}{\$50(1-0.15)} + 5.0\%$$

$$= \frac{\$4.40}{\$42.50} + 5.0\% = 15.4\%.$$

Copyright © 1996 by The Dryden Press. All rights reserved.

Flotation adjustment:

$$k_e - k_s = 15.4\% - 13.8\% = 1.6\%$$

Add the 1.6% flot. adj. to avg. k_s = 14% to find avg. k_e:

$$k_e = k_s + \text{Float adj.}$$
$$= 14\% + 1.6\% = \boxed{15.6\%.}$$

Why is $k_e > k_s$

1. **Investors expect to earn k_s.**

2. **Company gets money as RE; earns k_s; everything's O.K.**

3. **But investors put up money to buy new stock; F pulled out; so net money must earn > k_s to provide k_s on money investors put up.**

Example

1. $k_s = D_1/P_0 + g = 10\%$; F = 20%.
2. Investors put up $100, expect EPS = DPS = 0.1($100) = $10.
3. But company nets only $80.
4. If earn k_s = 10% on $80, EPS = DPS = 0.10(80) = $8. Too low. Price falls.
5. Need to earn k_e = 10%/0.8 = 12.5%.
6. Then EPS = 0.125(80) = $10.
   Conclusion: k_e = 12.5% > k_s = 10.0%.

BLUEPRINTS: CHAPTER 9
Copyright © 1996 by The Dryden Press. All rights reserved.

What's WACC using only RE for equity component of WACC$_1$?

$WACC_1 = w_d k_d (1-T) + w_{ps} k_{ps} + w_{ce} k_s$

$= 0.3(10\%)(0.6) + 0.1(9\%) + 0.6(14\%)$

$= 1.8\% + 0.9\% + 8.4\% = 11.1\%.$

= Cost per \$1 til R.E. used up.

WACC with new CS:

F = 15%:

$WACC_2 = w_d k_d (1-T) + w_{ps} k_{ps} + w_{ce} k_e$
$= 0.3(10\%)(0.6) + 0.1(9\%) + 0.6(15.6\%)$
$= 1.8 + 0.9 + 9.4 = 12.1\%.$

Summary to this point:

	k$_s$ or k$_e$	WACC
Debt + Pfd + R.E.:	14.0%	11.1%
Debt + Pfd + F = 15%:	15.6%	12.1%

WACC rises because equity cost is rising.

Copyright © 1996 by The Dryden Press. All rights reserved.

Define the MCC schedule.

- MCC shows cost of each dollar raised.

- Each dollar consists of $0.30 of debt, $0.10 of Pfd, and $0.60 of equity (RE or new CS).

- First dollars cost $WACC_1 = 11.1\%$, then $WACC_2 = 12.1\%$.

How large will capital budget be before must issue new CS?

Capital Budget = Capital Raised

$$Debt = 0.3 \text{ Cap. Raised}$$
$$Pfd = 0.1 \text{ Cap. Raised}$$
$$Equity = 0.6 \text{ Cap. Raised}$$
$$= 1.0 \text{ Total Cap.}$$

Equity = RE = 0.6 Cap. Raised, so
Cap. Raised = RE/0.6

Find <u>retained earnings break point</u>:

$$BP_{RE} = \frac{\text{Dollars of RE}}{\text{Fraction of equity}}$$

$$= \frac{\$300,000}{0.60} = \$500,000.$$

$500,000 total can be financed with R.E., debt, and Pfd.

BLUEPRINTS: CHAPTER 9
Copyright © 1996 by The Dryden Press. All rights reserved.

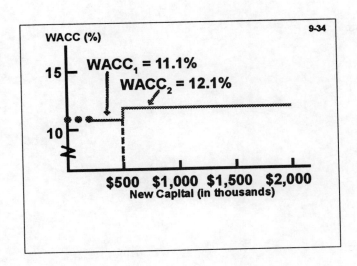

WACC (%)

WACC₁ = 11.1%

WACC₂ = 12.1%

15

10

$500 $1,000 $1,500 $2,000
New Capital (in thousands)

Investment Opportunities (Capital Budgeting Projects)

A	$ 700,000	17.0%
B	500,000	15.0%
C	800,000	11.5%
	$2,000,000	

Which to accept?

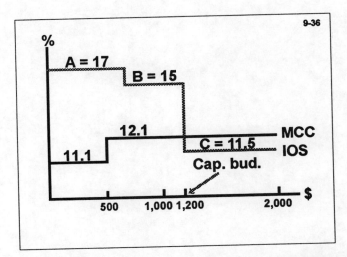

%

A = 17

B = 15

12.1

11.1

C = 11.5

MCC

IOS

Cap. bud.

500   1,000 1,200   2,000 $

Copyright © 1996 by The Dryden Press. All rights reserved.

- **Projects A and B would be accepted (IRR exceeds the MCC).**
- **Project C would be rejected (IRR is less than the MCC).**
- **Capital Budget = $1.2 million.**

Would the MCC remain constant beyond $2 million?

- **No.** WACC would eventually rise above 12.1%.
- Cost of debt, preferred stock would rise.
- Large increases in capital budget may also increase the perceived risk of the firm, increasing WACC.

Copyright © 1996 by The Dryden Press. All rights reserved.

EXAM-TYPE PROBLEMS

1. Barak Company's 8% coupon rate, quarterly payment, $1,000 par value bond, which matures in 20 years, currently sells at a price of $686.86. The company's tax rate is 40%. Based on the nominal interest rate, not the EAR, what is the firm's component cost of debt for purposes of calculating the WACC?

2. Allison Engines Corporation has established a target capital structure of 40% debt and 60% common equity. The firm expects to earn $600 in after-tax income during the coming year, and it will retain 40% of those earnings. The current market price of the firm's stock is P_0 = $28; its last dividend was D_0 = $2.20, and its expected dividend growth rate is 6%. Allison can issue new common stock at a flotation cost of 15%. What will Allison's marginal cost of *equity capital* (not the WACC) be if it must fund a capital budget requiring $600 in total new capital?

3. Gator Services Unlimited's (GSU) financial analyst must determine the firm's WACC for use in capital budgeting. She has gathered the following relevant data:

    (1)   Target capital structure: Debt 55%, Common equity 45%.

    (2)   Net income = $50 million; payout ratio = 40%.

    (3)   Interest rate on new debt = 10%.

    (4)   Flotation cost on all new stock issued = 15%.

    (5)   GSU's current stock price = $50.00; its last dividend was $3.00.

    (6)   The firm's constant growth rate is 10%; its tax rate is 35%.

    If GSU will raise $100 million, what will be its WACC?

Copyright © 1996 by The Dryden Press. All rights reserved.

10-17 Assume that you recently went to work for Allied Components Company, a supplier of auto repair parts used in the after-market with products from Chrysler, Ford, and other auto makers. Your boss, the chief financial officer (CFO), has just handed you the estimated cash flows for two proposed projects. Project L involves adding a new item to the firm's ignition system line; it would take some time to build up the market for this product, so the cash inflows would increase over time. Project S involves an add-on to an existing line, and its cash flows would decrease over time. Both projects have 3-year lives, because Allied is planning to introduce entirely new models after 3 years.

Here are the projects' net cash flows (in thousands of dollars):

	Expected Net Cash Flow	
Year	Project L	Project S
0	($100)	($100)
1	10	70
2	60	50
3	80	20

Depreciation, salvage values, net working capital requirements, and tax effects are all included in these cash flows.

The CFO also made subjective risk assessments of each project, and he concluded that the projects both have risk characteristics which are similar to the firm's average project. Allied's weighted average cost of capital is 10 percent. You must now determine whether one or both of the projects should be accepted.

a. What is capital budgeting? Are there any similarities between a firm's capital budgeting decisions and an individual's investment decisions?

b. What is the difference between independent and mutually exclusive projects? Between normal and nonnormal projects?

c. (1) What is the payback period? Find the paybacks for Projects L and S.

(2) What is the rationale for the payback method? According to the payback criterion, which project or projects should be accepted if the firm's maximum

Copyright © 1996 by The Dryden Press. All rights reserved.

acceptable payback is 2 years, and if Projects L and S are independent? If they are mutually exclusive?

    (3)   What is the difference between the regular payback and the discounted payback?

    (4)   What is the main disadvantage of discounted payback? Is the payback method of any real usefulness in capital budgeting decisions?

d. (1)   Define the term *net present value (NPV)*. What is each project's NPV?

    (2)   What is the rationale behind the NPV method? According to NPV, which project or projects should be accepted if they are independent? Mutually exclusive?

    (3)   Would the NPVs change if the cost of capital changed?

e. (1)   Define the term *internal rate of return (IRR)*. What is each project's IRR?

    (2)   How is the IRR on a project related to the YTM on a bond?

    (3)   What is the logic behind the IRR method? According to IRR, which projects should be accepted if they are independent? Mutually exclusive?

    (4)   Would the projects' IRRs change if the cost of capital changed?

f. (1)   Draw NPV profiles for Projects L and S. At what discount rate do the profiles cross?

    (2)   Look at your NPV profile graph without referring to the actual NPVs and IRRs. Which project or projects should be accepted if they are independent? Mutually exclusive? Explain. Are your answers correct at any cost of capital less than 23.6 percent?

g. (1)   What is the underlying cause of ranking conflicts between NPV and IRR?

    (2)   What is the "reinvestment rate assumption," and how does it affect the NPV versus IRR conflict?

    (3)   Which method is the best? Why?

h. (1)   Define the term *"modified IRR (MIRR)"*. Find the MIRRs for Projects L and S.

    (2)   What are the MIRR's advantages and disadvantages vis-a-vis the regular IRR? What are the MIRR's advantages and disadvantages vis-a-vis the NPV?

Copyright © 1996 by The Dryden Press. All rights reserved.

i. As a separate project (Project P), the firm is considering sponsoring a pavilion at the upcoming World's Fair. The pavilion would cost $800,000, and it is expected to result in $5 million of incremental cash inflows during its 1 year of operation. However, it would then take another year, and $5 million of costs, to demolish the site and return it to its original condition. Thus, Project P's expected net cash flows look like this (in millions of dollars):

Year	Net Cash Flows
0	($0.8)
1	5.0
2	(5.0)

The project is estimated to be of average risk, so its cost of capital is 10 percent.

(1)   What is Project P's NPV? What is its IRR? Its MIRR?

(2)   Draw Project P's NPV profile. Does Project P have normal or nonnormal cash flows? Should this project be accepted?

Copyright © 1996 by The Dryden Press. All rights reserved.

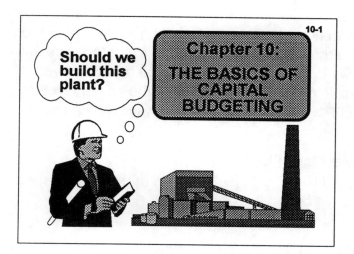

Should we build this plant?

Chapter 10:
THE BASICS OF CAPITAL BUDGETING

WHAT IS CAPITAL BUDGETING?

- Analysis of potential additions to fixed assets.

- Long-term decisions; involve large expenditures.

- Very important to firm's future.

Steps:

1. Estimate CFs (inflows & outflows).
2. Assess riskiness of CFs.
3. Determine k = WACC (adj.).
4. Find NPV and/or IRR.
5. Accept if NPV > 0 and/or IRR > WACC.

Copyright © 1996 by The Dryden Press. All rights reserved.

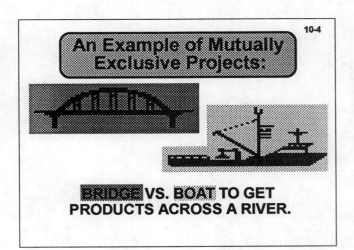

An Example of Mutually Exclusive Projects:

BRIDGE VS. BOAT TO GET
PRODUCTS ACROSS A RIVER.

Normal Project:

Cost (negative CF) followed by a
series of positive cash inflows.
One change of signs.

Nonnormal Project:

Two or more changes of signs.
Most common: Cost (negative
CF), then string of positive CFs,
then cost to close project.
Nuclear power plant, strip mine.

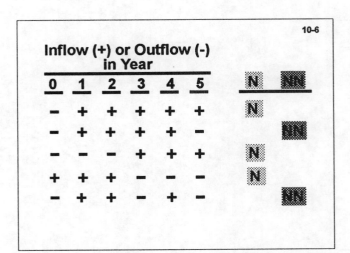

Inflow (+) or Outflow (-) in Year						N	NN
0	1	2	3	4	5		
–	+	+	+	+	+	N	
–	+	+	+	+	–		NN
–	–	–	+	+	+	N	
+	+	+	–	–	–	N	
–	+	+	–	+	–		NN

Copyright © 1996 by The Dryden Press. All rights reserved.

What is the payback period?

The number of years required to recover a project's cost,

or how long does it take to get our money back?

Payback for Project L (Long: Most CFs in out years)

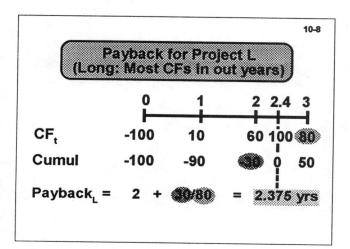

	0	1	2	2.4	3
CF_t	-100	10	60	100	80
Cumul	-100	-90		0	50

$Payback_L = 2 + 30/80 = 2.375$ yrs

Project S (Short: CFs come quickly)

	0	1	1.6	2	3
CF_t	-100	70	100	50	20
Cumul	-100		0	20	40

$Payback_s = 1 + 30/50 = 1.6$ yrs

Copyright © 1996 by The Dryden Press. All rights reserved.

Strengths of Payback:

1. Provides an indication of a project's **risk** and **liquidity**.
2. **Easy to calculate** and understand.

Weaknesses of Payback:

1. Ignores the **TVM**.
2. **Ignores CFs** occurring after the payback period.

Discounted payback: Uses discounted rather than raw CFs.

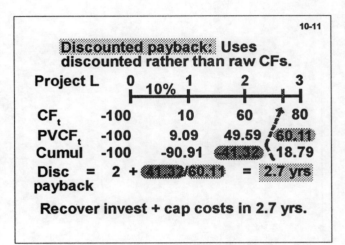

Project L	0	10%	1	2	3
CF_t	-100		10	60	80
$PVCF_t$	-100		9.09	49.59	60.11
Cumul	-100		-90.91	-41.32	18.79

Disc payback $= 2 + 41.32/60.11 = 2.7$ yrs

Recover invest + cap costs in 2.7 yrs.

NPV: Sum of the PVs of inflows and outflows.

$$NPV = \sum_{t=0}^{n} \frac{CF_t}{(1+k)^t}$$

Cost often is CF_0 and is **negative**.

$$NPV = \sum_{t=1}^{n} \frac{CF_t}{(1+k)^t} - CF_0$$

Copyright © 1996 by The Dryden Press. All rights reserved.

What's Project L's NPV?

Project L:

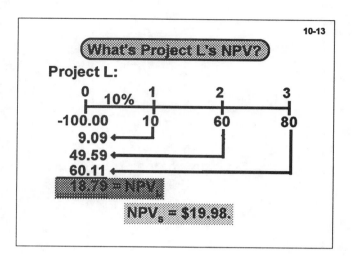

$NPV_s = \$19.98.$

Calculator Solution:

Enter in CFLO for L:

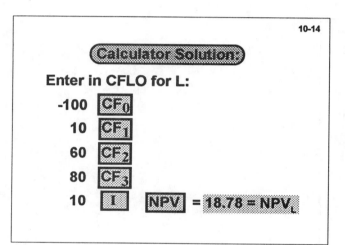

Rationale for the NPV method:

NPV = PV inflows - Cost
    = Net gain in wealth.

Accept project if NPV > 0.

Choose between mutually exclusive projects on basis of higher NPV. Adds most value.

Copyright © 1996 by The Dryden Press. All rights reserved.

Using NPV method, which project(s) should be accepted?

- If Projects S and L are **mutually exclusive**, accept S because $NPV_S > NPV_L$.

- If S & L are **independent**, accept both; NPV > 0.

Internal Rate of Return: IRR

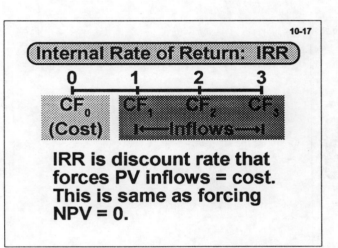

IRR is discount rate that forces PV inflows = cost. This is same as forcing NPV = 0.

NPV: Enter k, solve for NPV.

$$\sum_{t=0}^{n}\frac{CF_t}{(1+k)^t} = NPV.$$

IRR: Enter NPV = 0, solve for IRR.

$$\sum_{t=0}^{n}\frac{CF_t}{(1+IRR)^t} = 0.$$

Copyright © 1996 by The Dryden Press. All rights reserved.

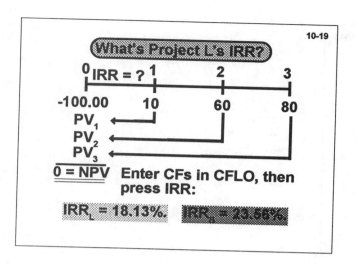

What's Project L's IRR?

0 IRR = ? 1   2   3

-100.00 10   60   80

PV_1 ←

PV_2 ←

PV_3 ←

0 = NPV **Enter CFs in CFLO, then press IRR:**

IRR_L = 18.13%. IRR_s = 23.56%

Find IRR if CFs are constant:

0 IRR = ? 1   2   3

-100   40   40   40

INPUTS	3		-100	40	0
	N	I/YR	PV	PMT	FV
OUTPUT		9.70%			

Or, with CFLO, enter CFs and press IRR = 9.70%.

Q. How is a project's IRR related to a bond's YTM?

A. They are the same thing. A bond's YTM is the IRR if you invest in the bond.

0 IRR=? 1   2   10

-1134.2 90   90   1090

IRR = 7.08% (use TVM or CFLO).

BLUEPRINTS: CHAPTER 10

Copyright © 1996 by The Dryden Press. All rights reserved.

Rationale for the IRR method:

If IRR > WACC, then the project's rate of return is greater than its cost-- some return is left over to boost stockholders' returns.
Example: WACC = 10%, IRR = 15%. Profitable.

IRR acceptance criteria:

- If IRR > k , **accept** project.

- If IRR < k, **reject** project.

Decisions on our Projects S and L per IRR:

- If S and L are **independent**, accept both. IRRs > k = 10%.

- If S and L are **mutually exclusive**, accept S because $IRR_s > IRR_L$.

Copyright © 1996 by The Dryden Press. All rights reserved.

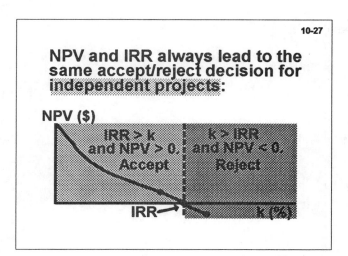

Copyright © 1996 by The Dryden Press. All rights reserved.

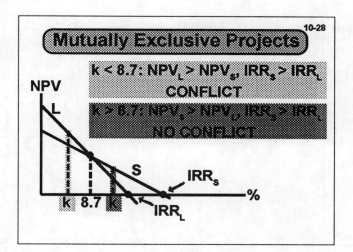

Mutually Exclusive Projects

10-28

k < 8.7: NPV$_L$ > NPV$_s$, IRR$_s$ > IRR$_L$
CONFLICT

k > 8.7: NPV$_s$ > NPV$_L$, IRR$_s$ > IRR$_L$
NO CONFLICT

To find the crossover rate:

10-29

1. **Find cash flow differences between the projects. See data at beginning of the case.**

2. **Enter these differences in CFLO register, then press IRR. Crossover rate = 8.68 rounded to 8.7%.**

3. **Can subtract S from L or vice versa, but better to have first CF negative.**

4. **If profiles don't cross, one project dominates the other.**

Two reasons NPV profiles cross:

10-30

1) **Size (scale) differences.** Smaller project frees up funds at t = 0 for investment. The higher the opp. cost, the more valuable these funds, so high k favors small projects.

2) **Timing differences.** Project with faster payback provides more CF in early years for reinvestment. If k is high, early CF especially good, NPV$_s$ > NPV$_L$.

Copyright © 1996 by The Dryden Press. All rights reserved.

Reinvestment Rate Assumptions

- NPV assumes reinvest at k (opp. cost of capital).

- IRR assumes reinvest at IRR.

- Reinvest at opp. cost, k, is more realistic, so NPV method is best. NPV should be used to choose between mutually exclusive projects.

Managers like rates--prefer IRR to NPV comparisons. Can we give them a better IRR?

Yes. MIRR is the discount rate which causes the PV of a project's terminal value (TV) to equal the PV of costs. TV is found by compounding inflows at WACC.

Thus, MIRR assumes cash inflows are reinvested at WACC.

MIRR for Project L (k = 10%):

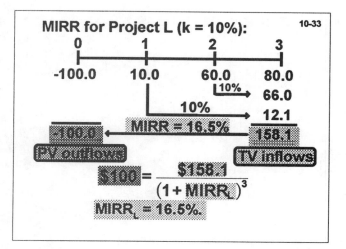

$$\$100 = \frac{\$158.1}{(1 + MIRR_L)^3}$$

$MIRR_L = 16.5\%.$

Copyright © 1996 by The Dryden Press. All rights reserved.

To find TV with 10B, enter in CFLO:

$CF_0 = 0$, $CF_1 = 10$, $CF_2 = 60$, $CF_3 = 80$

$I = 10$

NPV = 118.78 = (PV) of inflows.

Now enter (PV) = -118.78, N = 3, I = 10, PMT = 0.

Press (FV) = 158.10 = FV of inflows.

Now enter FV = 158.10, PV = -100, PMT=0, N=3.

Press I = (16.50% = MIRR.)

Why use MIRR versus IRR?

MIRR correctly assumes reinvestment at opp. cost = WACC. MIRR also avoids the problem of multiple IRRs.

Managers like rate of return comparisons, and MIRR is better for this than IRR.

Pavilion Project: NPV and IRR?

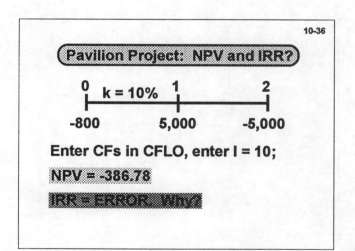

```
0       k = 10%    1              2
|------------------|--------------|
-800              5,000         -5,000
```

Enter CFs in CFLO, enter I = 10;

NPV = -386.78

IRR = ERROR. Why?

Copyright © 1996 by The Dryden Press. All rights reserved.

We got IRR = ERROR because there are 2 IRRs. Nonnormal CFs--two sign changes. Here's a picture:

NPV Profile

NPV

450

0

-800

100

400

k

$IRR_2 = 400\%$

$IRR_1 = 25\%$

Logic of Multiple IRRs:

1. At very low disc. rates, the PV of CF_2 is large & negative, so NPV<0.

2. At very high disc. rates, the PV of CF_1 and CF_2 are both low, so CF_0 dominates and again NPV<0.

3. In between, the disc. rate hits CF_2 harder than CF_1, so NPV>0.

4. Result: 2 IRRs.

Could find IRR with calculator:

1. Enter CFs as before.

2. Enter a "guess" as to IRR by storing the guess. Try 10%:

    10 ■ STO

    ■ IRR = 25% = lower IRR

Now guess large IRR, say, 200:

    200 ■ STO

    ■ IRR = 400% = upper IRR

Copyright © 1996 by The Dryden Press. All rights reserved.

When there are nonnormal CFs and more than one IRR, use MIRR:

```
        0              1              2
        |_____|_____|
```

-800,000   5,000,000   -5,000,000

PV outflows @10% = -4,932,231.40.

TV inflows @10% = 5,500,000.00.

MIRR = 5.6%.

Accept Project P?

No. Reject because MIRR = 5.6% < k = 10%.

Also, if MIRR < k, NPV will be negative: NPV = -$386,777.

Copyright © 1996 by The Dryden Press. All rights reserved.

EXAM-TYPE PROBLEMS

1. A company is analyzing two mutually exclusive projects, S and L, whose cash flows are shown below:

Years	0	1	2	3	4
S	-1,100	900	350	50	10
L	-1,100	0	300	500	850

The company's cost of capital is 12 percent, and it can get an unlimited amount of capital at that cost. What is the *regular IRR* (not MIRR) of the *better* project? (Hint: Note that the better project may or may not be the one with the higher IRR.)

2. As the director of capital budgeting for Lasser Company, you are evaluating two mutually exclusive projects with the following net cash flows:

Year	Project X	Project Z
0	-$100	-$100
1	50	10
2	40	30
3	30	40
4	10	60

Is there a crossover point in the relevant part of the NPV profile graph (the upper right quadrant) and, if there is, at what rate does it occur?

3. Below are the returns of Nulook Cosmetics and the "market" over a three-year period:

Year	Nulook	Market
1	9%	6%
2	15%	10%
3	36%	24%

Nulook finances internally using only retained earnings, and it uses the Capital Asset Pricing Model with a historical beta to determine its cost of equity. Currently, the risk-free rate is 7%, and the estimated market risk premium is 6%. Nulook is evaluating a project which has a cost today of $2,028 and will provide estimated cash inflows of $1,000 at the end of each of the next 3 years. What is this project's MIRR?

BLUEPRINTS: CHAPTER 10
Copyright © 1996 by The Dryden Press. All rights reserved.

11-13 After seeing Snapple's success with noncola soft drinks and learning of Coke's and Pepsi's interest, Allied Food Products has decided to consider an expansion of its own in the fruit juice business. The product being considered is fresh lemon juice. Assume that you were recently hired as assistant to the director of capital budgeting, and you must evaluate the new project.

The lemon juice would be produced in an unused building adjacent to Allied's Fort Myers plant; Allied owns the building, which is fully depreciated. The required equipment would cost $200,000, plus an additional $40,000 for shipping and installation. In addition, inventories would rise by $25,000, while accounts payable would go up by $5,000. All of these costs would be incurred at t = 0. By a special ruling, the machinery could be depreciated under the MACRS system as 3-year property.

The project is expected to operate for 4 years, at which time it will be terminated. The cash inflows are assumed to begin 1 year after the project is undertaken, or at t = 1, and to continue out to t = 4. At the end of the project's life (t = 4), the equipment is expected to have a salvage value of $25,000.

Unit sales are expected to total 100,000 cans per year, and the expected sales price is $2.00 per can. Cash operating costs for the project (total operating costs less depreciation) are expected to total 60 percent of dollar sales. Allied's tax rate is 40 percent, and its weighted average cost of capital is 10 percent. Tentatively, the lemon juice project is assumed to be of equal risk to Allied's other assets.

You have been asked to evaluate the project and to make a recommendation as to whether it should be accepted or rejected. To guide you in your analysis, your boss gave you the following set of questions.

a. Draw a time line which shows when the net cash inflows and outflows will occur, and explain how the time line can be used to help structure the analysis.

b. Allied has a standard form which is used in the capital budgeting process; see Table IC11-1. Part of the table has been completed, but you must replace the blanks with the missing numbers.

Copyright © 1996 by The Dryden Press. All rights reserved.

Table IC11-1. Allied's Lemon Juice Project
(Total Cost in Thousands)

End of Year:	0	1	2	3	4
Unit sales (thousands)			100		
Price/unit		$ 2.00	$ 2.00		
Total revenues					$200.0
Operating costs, excluding depreciation			$120.0		
Depreciation				36.0	16.8
Total costs		$199.2	$228.0		
EBT				$44.0	
Taxes		0.3			25.3
Net income				$26.4	
Depreciation		79.2		36.0	
Net operating cash flow	$ 0.0	$ 79.7			$ 54.7
Equipment cost					
Installation					
Increase in inventory					
Increase in accounts payable					
Salvage value					
Tax on salvage value					
Return of net working capital					
Time line (net cash flow):	($260.0)				$ 89.7
Cumulative cash flow for payback:	(260.0)	(180.3)			63.0
Compounded inflows for MIRR:		106.1			89.7
Terminal value of inflows:					
NPV =					
IRR =					
MIRR =					
Payback =					

Copyright © 1996 by The Dryden Press. All rights reserved.

Complete the table in the following steps:

(1)   Complete the table for unit sales, sales price, total revenues, and operating costs excluding depreciation.

(2)   Complete the depreciation data.

(3)   Now complete the table down to net income, and then down to net operating cash flows.

(4)   Now fill in the blanks under Year 0 and Year 4, for the initial cost and the termination cash flows, and complete the "time line (net cash flow)" line. Discuss working capital. What would have happened if the machinery were sold for less than its book value?

c. (1)   Allied uses debt in its capital structure, so some of the money used to finance the project will be debt. Given this fact, should the projected cash flows be revised to show projected interest charges? Explain.

(2)   Suppose you learned that Allied had spent $50,000 to renovate the building last year, expensing these costs. Should this cost be reflected in the analysis? Explain.

(3)   Now suppose you learned that Allied could lease its building to another party and earn $25,000 per year. Should that fact be reflected in the analysis? If so, how?

(4)   Now assume that the lemon juice project would take away profitable sales from Allied's fresh orange juice business. Should that fact be reflected in your analysis? If so, how?

d. Disregard all the assumptions made in Part c, and assume there was no alternative use for the building over the next 4 years. Now calculate the project's NPV, IRR, MIRR, and regular payback. Do these indicators suggest that the project should be accepted?

e. If this project had been a replacement rather than an expansion project, how would the analysis have changed? Think about the changes that would have to occur in the cash flow table.

f. Assume that inflation is expected to average 5 percent over the next 4 years; that this expectation is reflected in the WACC; and that inflation will increase variable costs and revenues by the same percentage, 5 percent. Does it appear that inflation has been dealt with properly in the analysis? If not, what should be done, and how would the

Copyright © 1996 by The Dryden Press. All rights reserved.

required adjustment affect the decision? You can modify the numbers in the table to quantify your results.

g. In an unrelated analysis, you have also been asked to choose between the following two mutually exclusive projects:

	Expected Net Cash Flows	
Year	Project S	Project L
0	($100,000)	($100,000)
1	60,000	33,500
2	60,000	33,500
3	--	33,500
4	--	33,500

The projects provide a necessary service, so whichever one is selected is expected to be repeated into the foreseeable future. Both projects are of average risk.

(1) What is each project's initial NPV without replication?

(2) Now construct a time line, and then apply the replacement chain approach to determine the projects' extended NPVs. Which project should be chosen?

(3) Repeat the analysis using the equivalent annual annuity approach.

(4) Now assume that the cost to repeat Project S in Year 2 will increase to $105,000 because of inflationary pressures. How should the analysis be handled now, and which project should be chosen?

11-14 Ron Redwine, financial manager of Blum Industries, is developing the firm's optimal capital budget for the coming year. He has identified the five potential projects shown below; none of the projects can be repeated. Projects B and B* are mutually exclusive, while the remainder are independent.

Project	Cost	CF_{1-n}	Life (n)	IRR	NPV
A	$400,000	$119,326	5	15%	
B	200,000	56,863	5	13	
B*	200,000	35,397	10	12	
C	100,000	27,057	5	11	
D	300,000	79,139	5	10	

Copyright © 1996 by The Dryden Press. All rights reserved.

The following information was developed for use in determining Blum's weighted average cost of capital (WACC):

Interest rate on new debt	8.0%
Tax rate	40.0%
Debt ratio	60.0%
Current stock price, P_0	$20.00
Last dividend, D_0	$2.00
Expected growth rate, g	6.0%
Flotation cost on common, F	19.0%
Expected addition to retained earnings	$200,000.00

Blum adjusts for differential project risk by adding or subtracting 2 percentage points to the firm's marginal cost of capital.

a. Calculate the WACC, and then plot the company's IOS and MCC schedules. What is the firm's marginal cost of capital for capital budgeting purposes?

b. Assume initially that all five projects are of average risk. What is Blum's optimal capital budget? Explain your answer.

c. Now assume that the retained earnings break point occurred at $900,000 of new capital. What effect would this have on the firm's MCC schedule and on its optimal capital budget?

d. Return to the situation in Part a, with the $500,000 retained earnings break point. Suppose Project A is reexamined, and it is judged to be a high-risk project, while Projects C and D are, upon reexamination, judged to have low risk. Projects B and B* remain average-risk projects. How would these changes affect Blum's optimal capital budget?

e. In reality, companies like Blum have hundreds of projects to evaluate each year; hence it is generally not practical to draw the IOS and MCC schedules which include every potential project. Suppose this situation exists for Blum. Suppose also that the company has 3 divisions, L, A, and H, with low, average, and high risk, respectively, and that the projects within each division can also be grouped into three risk categories. Describe how Blum might go about structuring its capital budgeting decision process and choosing its optimal set of projects. For this purpose, assume that Blum's overall WACC is estimated to be 11 percent. As part of your answer, find appropriate divisional and project hurdle rates when differential risk is considered.

Copyright © 1996 by The Dryden Press. All rights reserved.

CHAPTER 11
Risk and Other Topics in Capital Budgeting

- Relevant Cash Flows
- Working Capital in Cap. Bud.
- Unequal Project Lives
- Inflation
- Optimal Capital Budget

Proposed Project:

- Cost: $200,000 + $10,000 shipping + $30,000 installation. Depreciable cost: $240,000.
- Inventories will rise by $25,000 and payables by $5,000.
- Economic life = 4 years.
- Salvage value = $25,000.
- MACRS 3-year class.

- Sales: 100,000 units/yr @ $2.

- Var. cost = 60% of sales.

- Tax rate = 40%.

- WACC = 10%.

BLUEPRINTS: CHAPTER 11
Copyright © 1996 by The Dryden Press. All rights reserved.

11-4

Set up, without numbers, a time line for the project's cash flows:

0	1	2	3	4
Initial Costs (CF_0)	OCF_1	OCF_2	OCF_3	OCF_4 + Terminal CF
NCF_0	NCF_1	NCF_2	NCF_3	NCF_4

11-5

What's the annual depreciation?

Year	Rate	x	Basis	Depreciation
1	0.33		$240	$ 79
2	0.45		240	108
3	0.15		240	36
4	0.07		240	17
	1.00			$240

Due to 1/2-yr conv., a 3-yr asset is depreciated over 4 years.

11-6

Operating cash flows:

	1	2	3	4
Revenues	$200	$200	$200	$200
Op. Cost, 60%	-120	-120	-120	-120
Depr'n	-79	-108	-36	-17
EBT	1	-28	44	63
Tax, 40%	--	-11	18	25
NI	1	-17	26	38
Add. Depr'n	79	108	36	17
Op. CF	80	91	62	55

Copyright © 1996 by The Dryden Press. All rights reserved.

Investment at t = 0:

Equipment	-$200
Installation & Ship.	-40
Increase in inv.	-25
Increase in A/P	5
Net CF_0	-$260

NWC = $25 - $5 = $20.

Net Terminal CF at t = 4:

Salvage value	$25
Tax on SV (40%)	-10
Recovery of NWC	20
Net termination CF	$35

Q. Always a tax on SV? Ever a positive tax number?

Q. How is NWC recovered?

Should CFs include int. expense? Dividends?

- **No.** The cost of capital is accounted for by discounting at the 10% WACC, so deducting interest and dividends would be "double counting" financing costs.

Copyright © 1996 by The Dryden Press. All rights reserved.

Suppose $50,000 had been spent last year to improve the building. Should this cost be included in the analysis?

No. This is a sunk cost. Analyze incremental investment.

Suppose the plant could be leased out for $25,000 a year. Would this affect the analysis?

- Yes. Accepting the project means foregoing the $25,000. This is an opportunity cost, and it should be charged to the project.

- A.T. opp cost = $25,000 (1 - T) = $25,000 (0.6) = $15,000 annual cost.

If the new product line would decrease sales of the firm's other lines, would this affect the analysis?

- Yes. The effects on other projects' CFs is an "externality."

- Net CF loss per year on other lines would be a cost to this project.

- Externalities can be positive or neg. i.e., complements or substitutes.

Copyright © 1996 by The Dryden Press. All rights reserved.

Here are all the project's net CFs (in thousands) on a time line:

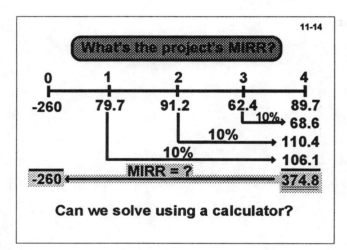

What's the project's MIRR?

Can we solve using a calculator?

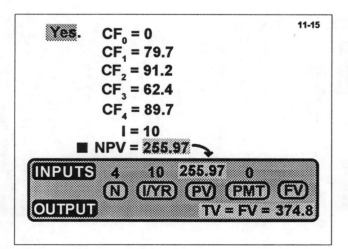

Copyright © 1996 by The Dryden Press. All rights reserved.

11-16

Use the FV = TV of inputs to find MIRR:

INPUTS	4		-260	0	374.8
	(N)	(I/YR)	(PV)	(PMT)	(FV)
OUTPUT		9.6			

MIRR = 9.6%. Since MIRR < k = 10%, reject the project.

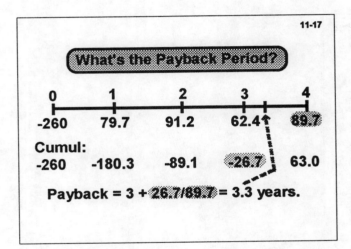

11-17

What's the Payback Period?

0	1	2	3	4
-260	79.7	91.2	62.4	89.7

Cumul:

| -260 | -180.3 | -89.1 | -26.7 | 63.0 |

Payback = 3 + 26.7/89.7 = 3.3 years.

11-18

If this were a replacement rather than a new project, would the analysis change?

Yes. The old equipment would be sold, and the incremental CFs would be the **changes** from the old to the new situation.

Copyright © 1996 by The Dryden Press. All rights reserved.

- **The relevant deprn. would be the change with the new equipment.**

- **Also, if the firm sold the old machine now, it would not receive the SV at the end of the machine's life.**

Q. If E(INFL) = 5%, is NPV biased?

A. Yes. $NPV = \sum_{t=0}^{N} \frac{CF_t}{(1+k)^t} = \frac{Rev_t - Cost_t}{(1+k)^t}$.

$k = k^* + IP + DRP + LP + MRP$.

Inflation is in denominator but not in numerator, so downward bias to NPV.

Should build inflation into CF forecasts.

S and L are mutually exclusive and will be repeated. k = 10%. Which is better?

Expected Net CFs:

Year	Project S	Project L
0	($100,000)	($100,000)
1	60,000	33,500
2	60,000	33,500
3	--	33,500
4	--	33,500

Copyright © 1996 by The Dryden Press. All rights reserved.

	S	L
CF_0	-100,000	-100,000
CF_1	60,000	33,500
N_j	2	4
I	10	10
NPV	4,132	6,190

Q. $NPV_L > NPV_S$. Is L better?

A. Can't say. Need replacement chain analysis.

- Note that Project S could be repeated after 2 years to generate additional profits.
- Use replacement chain to calculate extended NPV_S to a common life.
- Since S has a 2-yr life and L a 4-yr life, the common life is 4 yrs.

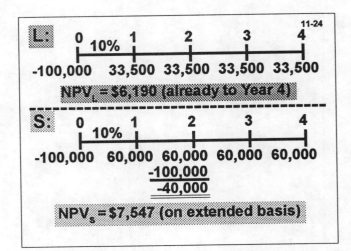

L:

```
0        1        2        3        4
  10%
-100,000  33,500  33,500  33,500  33,500
```

NPV_L = $6,190 (already to Year 4)

- -

S:

```
0        1        2        3        4
  10%
-100,000  60,000   60,000   60,000   60,000
                   -100,000
                    -40,000
```

NPV_S = $7,547 (on extended basis)

Copyright © 1996 by The Dryden Press. All rights reserved.

Equivalent annual annuity:
That annuity PMT whose PV equals the project's NPV.

S:

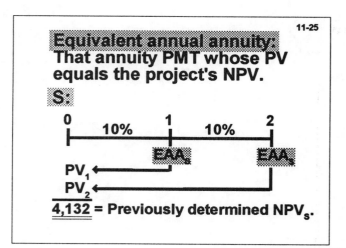

0   10%   1   10%   2

EAA$_s$ EAA$_s$

PV$_1$ ←

PV$_2$ ←

4,132 = Previously determined NPV$_s$.

Project S (EAA):

INPUTS   2   10   -4132   0

N   I/YR   PV   PMT   FV

OUTPUT   EAA$_s$ = 2380.82

Project L (EAA):

INPUTS   4   10   -6190   0

N   I/YR   PV   PMT   FV

OUTPUT   EAA$_L$ = 1952.76

The higher annuity is better.

- The project, in effect, provides an annuity of EAA.

- EAA$_S$ > EAA$_L$, so pick S.

- Replacement chains and EAA always lead to the same decision.

Copyright © 1996 by The Dryden Press. All rights reserved.

If the cost to repeat S in two years rises to $105,000, which would be best?

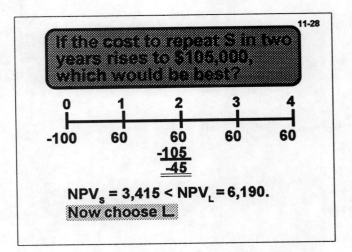

0	1	2	3	4
-100	60	60	60	60

$$-105$$
$$-45$$

NPV$_S$ = 3,415 < NPV$_L$ = 6,190.
Now choose L

Part 2: The Optimal Capital Budget

- We've seen how to evaluate projects.
- We need cost of capital for evaluation.
- But WACC depends on size of capital budget.
- Must combine WACC and capital budget analysis.

Blum Industries has 5 potential projects:

Project	Cost	CF	Life (N)	IRR
A	$400,000	$119,326	5	15%
B	200,000	56,863	5	13
B*	200,000	35,397	10	12
C	100,000	27,057	5	11
D	300,000	79,139	5	10

Projects B & B* are mutually exclusive, the others are independent. Neither B nor B* will be repeated.

BLUEPRINTS: CHAPTER 11

Copyright © 1996 by The Dryden Press. All rights reserved.

Additional information:

Interest rate on new debt	8.0%
Tax rate	40.0%
Debt ratio	60.0%
Current stock price, P_0	$20.00
Last dividend, D_0	$2.00
Expected growth rate, g	6.0%
Flotation cost on CS, F	19.0%
Expected addition to RE	$200,000
(NI = $500,000, Payout = 60%)	

For differential project risk, add or subtract 2% to WACC.

Calculate WACC, then plot IOS and MCC schedules.

Step 1: Estimate the cost of equity:

$$k_s = \frac{D_0(1+g)}{P_0} + g = \frac{\$2(1.06)}{\$20} + 6\% = 16.6\%$$

$$k_e = \frac{D_1}{P_0(1-F)} + g = \frac{\$2(1.06)}{\$20(1-0.19)} + 6\%$$

$$= \frac{\$2.12}{\$16.2} + 6\% = 19.1\%$$

Step 2: Estimate the WACCs

$$WACC_1 = w_d k_d (1-T) + w_{ce} k_s$$
$$= (0.6)(8\%)(0.6)$$
$$+ 0.4(16.6\%) = 9.5\%.$$

$$WACC_2 = w_d k_d (1-T) + w_{ce} k_e$$
$$= (0.6)(8\%)(0.6)$$
$$+ 0.4(19.1\%) = 10.5\%.$$

Copyright © 1996 by The Dryden Press. All rights reserved.

Step 3: Estimate the RE break point

$$BP_{RE} = \frac{\text{Retained earnings}}{\text{Equity fraction}}$$

$$= \frac{\$200,000}{0.4} = \$500,000.$$

Each dollar up to $500,000 has $0.40 of R.E. at cost of 16.6%, then WACC rises.

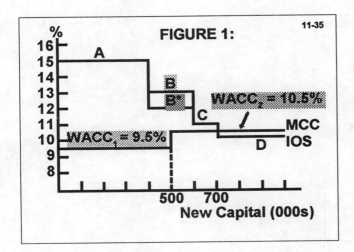

FIGURE 1:

- The IOS schedule plots projects in descending order of IRR.

- Two potential IOS schedules--one with A, B, C, and D, and another with A, B*, C, and D.

- The WACC has a break point at $500,000 of new capital.

BLUEPRINTS: CHAPTER 11

Copyright © 1996 by The Dryden Press. All rights reserved.

What MCC do we use for capital budgeting, i.e., for calculating NPV?

- **MCC:** WACC that exists where IOS and MCC schedules intersect. In this case, MCC = 10.5%.

If all 5 projects are average risk, what's the optimal capital budget?

- **MCC = 10.5%.**

- IRR and NPV lead to same decisions for independent projects. Thus, all independent projects with IRRs above 10.5% should be accepted.

- Therefore, accept A and C, reject D and accept B or B*.

- NPV and IRR can conflict for mutually exclusive projects.

- NPV method is better, so choose between B and B* based on NPV at WACC = 10.5%.

- $NPV_{B*} = \$12,905 > NPV_B = \$12,830$, so choose B* over B.

Copyright © 1996 by The Dryden Press. All rights reserved.

Suppose you aren't sure of WACC. At what WACC would B and B* have the same NPV?

Get differences:

$CF_0 = 200,000 - 200,000 = \qquad 0$

$CF_{1-5} = 56,863 - 35,397 = 21,466$

$CF_{6-10} = 0 - 35,397 \qquad = -35,397$

Indifference WACC = IRR = 10.52%.

The risk-adjusted rates are as follows:

WACC = 10.5% ± 2%

Project Risk	Risk-Adjusted Hurdle Rate
Low: C, D	8.5%
Average: B, B*	10.5
High: A	12.5

	IRR	Hurdle Rate	
A	15%	12.5%	Accept
B	13	10.5	Accept ⎤ one
B*	12	10.5	Accept ⎦
C	11	8.5	Accept
D	10	8.5	Accept

Now the optimal capital budget consists of A, B (or B*), C, and D, for a total of $1,000,000.

WACC is still = 10.5%, so NPV_{B*} still larger than NPV_B.

BLUEPRINTS: CHAPTER 11

Copyright © 1996 by The Dryden Press. All rights reserved.

EXAM-TYPE PROBLEMS

1. McQueen Corporation is considering two mutually exclusive projects which are expected to generate the following cash flows:

   The two projects are not repeatable. McQueen evaluates investment projects with close to equal lives, such as these, only with the NPV method. At what cost of capital should McQueen be indifferent between the two projects?

2. Far West Airlines seeks to purchase one of two alternative jetliners. Jet A costs $2 million, has an expected life of 7 years, and will generate net cash flows of $520,000 per year. An identical Jet A can be purchased for the same price when the first jet's life is over. Jet B costs $6.2 million, has an expected life of 14 years, and is expected to produce net cash flows of $1,012,000 per year. Assume that inflation in operating costs, airplane expenditures, and fares will be zero, that the cash inflows occur at the end of the year, and that the firm's cost of capital is 12%. If the firm chooses the jet project that will add the most value to the firm, by how much will the company's value increase?

3. Career Training Associates (CTA) has a debt ratio of 20 percent. Management has concluded that this capital structure is optimal. CTA has analyzed its investment opportunities for the coming year and has identified four possible additions to assets which generate IRRs greater than zero.

Investment	Size	IRR
A	$ 3 Million	20.1%
B	6 Million	18.8
C	12 Million	19.2
D	9 Million	18.0

   CTA is forecasting net income for the coming year of $10 million and expects to pay out 50 percent in dividends to the 1 million outstanding shares of common stock. The earnings have been growing at a constant rate of 10 percent over the past few years,

Copyright © 1996 by The Dryden Press. All rights reserved.

and this rate is expected to continue indefinitely. If CTA has to sell new common stock, it will be faced with flotation costs of 15 percent. The current market price of the stock is $50 per share. Any debt that is raised will require a coupon rate of 8 percent. The marginal tax rate is 34 percent. How large will CTA's capital budget be if all investments with an IRR greater than the MCC are accepted?

4. If a typical U.S. company uses the same discount rate to evaluate all projects, the firm will most likely become

   a. Riskier over time, and its value will decline.

   b. Riskier over time, and its value will rise.

   c. Less risky over time, and its value will rise.

   d. Less risky over time, and its value will decline.

   e. There is no reason to expect its risk position or value to change over time as a result of its use of a single discount rate.

5. Envirotech Company issued $10,000,000 in $1,000 par value, 15% coupon bonds 10 years ago. When issued, the bonds had 30 years to maturity, paid interest semiannually, and were callable at a call premium of $100 each. Market interest rates are now 13.5%. Envirotech can issue new bonds at current market rates with a $1,000 par value, 20 year maturity, and semiannual payments which would replace the old issue, for flotation costs of $400,000. Assume that the firm has a marginal tax rate of zero percent and that all flotation costs will be treated as a lump sum cost incurred at time = 0 (i.e., there are no tax effects). What is the NPV of this refunding project? (Hint: See Appendix 11B.)

Copyright © 1996 by The Dryden Press. All rights reserved.

12-14 Assume that you have just been hired as business manager of Campus Deli (CD), which is located adjacent to the campus. Sales were $1,350,000 last year; variable costs were 60 percent of sales; and fixed costs were $40,000. Therefore, EBIT totaled $500,000. Because the university's enrollment is capped, EBIT is expected to be constant over time. Since no expansion capital is required, CD pays out all earnings as dividends. Assets are $2 million, and 100,000 shares are outstanding. The management group owns about 50 percent of the stock, which is traded in the over-the-counter market.

CD currently has no debt—it is an all-equity firm—and its 100,000 shares outstanding sell at a price of $20 per share, which is also the book value. The firm's federal-plus-state tax rate is 40 percent. On the basis of statements made in your finance text, you believe that CD's shareholders would be better off if some debt financing were used. When you suggested this to your new boss, she encouraged you to pursue the idea, but to provide support for the suggestion.

You then obtained from a local investment banker the following estimates of the costs of debt and equity at different debt levels (in thousands of dollars):

Amount Borrowed	k_d	k_s
$ 0	10.0%	15.0%
250	10.0	15.5
500	11.0	16.5
750	13.0	18.0
1,000	16.0	20.0

If the firm were recapitalized, debt would be issued, and the borrowed funds would be used to repurchase stock. Stockholders, in turn, would use funds provided by the repurchase to buy equities in other fast-food companies similar to CD. You plan to complete your report by asking and then answering the following questions.

a. (1)   What is business risk? What factors influence a firm's business risk?

(2)   What is operating leverage, and how does it affect a firm's business risk?

b. (1)   What is meant by the terms "financial leverage" and "financial risk"?

(2)   How does financial risk differ from business risk?

Copyright © 1996 by The Dryden Press. All rights reserved.

c. Now, to develop an example which can be presented to CD's management as an illustration, consider two hypothetical firms, Firm U, with zero debt financing, and Firm L, with $10,000 of 12 percent debt. Both firms have $20,000 in total assets and a 40 percent federal-plus-state tax rate, and they have the following EBIT probability distribution for next year:

Probability	EBIT
0.25	$2,000
0.50	3,000
0.25	4,000

(1) Complete the partial income statements and the firms' ratios in Table IC12-1.

Table IC12-1. Income Statements and Ratios

	Firm U			Firm L		
Assets	$20,000	$20,000	$20,000	$20,000	$20,000	$20,000
Equity	$20,000	$20,000	$20,000	$10,000	$10,000	$10,000
Probability	0.25	0.50	0.25	0.25	0.50	0.25
Sales	$ 6,000	$ 9,000	$12,000	$ 6,000	$ 9,000	$12,000
Oper. costs	4,000	6,000	8,000	4,000	6,000	8,000
EBIT	$ 2,000	$ 3,000	$ 4,000	$ 2,000	$ 3,000	$ 4,000
Int. (12%)	0	0	0	1,200		1,200
EBT	$ 2,000	$ 3,000	$ 4,000	$ 800	$	$ 2,800
Taxes (40%)	800	1,200	1,600	320		1,120
Net income	$ 1,200	$ 1,800	$ 2,400	$ 480	$	$ 1,680
BEP	10.0%	15.0%	20.0%	10.0%	%	20.0%
ROE	6.0%	9.0%	12.0%	4.8%	%	16.8%
TIE	∞	∞	∞	1.7×	×	3.3×
E(BEP)		15.0%			%	
E(ROE)		9.0%			10.8%	
E(TIE)		∞			2.5×	
σ(BEP)		3.5%			%	
σ(ROE)		2.1%			4.2%	
σ(TIE)		0			0.6×	

Copyright © 1996 by The Dryden Press. All rights reserved.

(2)   Be prepared to discuss each entry in the table and to explain how this example illustrates the impact of financial leverage on expected rate of return and risk.

d. With the above points in mind, now consider the optimal capital structure for CD.

(1)   To begin, define the terms "optimal capital structure" and "target capital structure."

(2)   Describe briefly, without using numbers, the sequence of events that would occur if CD decided to recapitalize and to increase its use of debt.

(3)   Assume that shares could be repurchased at the current market price of $20 per share. Calculate CD's expected EPS and TIE at debt levels of $0, $250,000, $500,000, $750,000, and $1,000,000. How many shares would remain after recapitalization under each scenario?

(4)   What would be the new stock price if CD recapitalizes with $250,000 of debt? $500,000? $750,000? $1,000,000? Recall that the payout ratio is 100 percent, so g = 0.

(5)   Considering only the levels of debt discussed, what is CD's optimal capital structure?

(6)   Is EPS maximized at the debt level which maximizes share price? Why?

(7)   What is the WACC at the optimal capital structure?

e. Suppose you discovered that CD had more business risk than you originally estimated. Describe how this would affect the analysis. What if the firm had less business risk than originally estimated?

f.   What is meant by the terms "degree of operating leverage (DOL)", "degree of financial leverage (DFL)", and "degree of total leverage (DTL)"? If fixed costs total $40,000 and the company uses $500,000 of debt, what are CD's degrees of each type of leverage? Of what practical use is the degree of leverage concept?

g. What are some factors a manager should consider when establishing his or her firm's target capital structure?

h. Put labels on Figure IC12-1, and then discuss the graph as you might use it to explain to your boss why CD might want to use some debt.

Copyright © 1996 by The Dryden Press. All rights reserved.

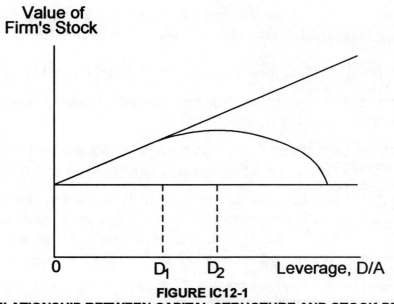

Value of
Firm's Stock

0   D₁   D₂   Leverage, D/A

FIGURE IC12-1
RELATIONSHIP BETWEEN CAPITAL STRUCTURE AND STOCK PRICE

i. How does the existence of asymmetric information and signaling affect capital structure?

Copyright © 1996 by The Dryden Press. All rights reserved.

CHAPTER 12
Capital Structure and Leverage

- **Business vs. Financial Risk**
- **Optimal Capital Structure**
- **Degree of Leverage**
- **Capital Structure Theory**

What is Business Risk?

- **Uncertainty about future operating income (EBIT). How well can we predict operating income?**

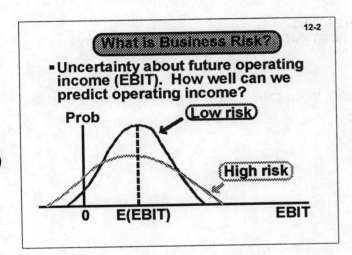

Business risk is affected primarily by:

(1) Uncertainty about demand (sales).

(2) Uncertainty about output prices.

(3) Uncertainty about costs.

(4) Product, other liability.

(5) Degree of operating leverage (DOL).

Copyright © 1996 by The Dryden Press. All rights reserved.

What is operating leverage, and how does it affect a firm's business risk?

- **Operating leverage:** Use of fixed rather than variable costs.
- If most costs are fixed, hence do not decline when demand falls, then firm has a **high DOL.**

- More op. lev. leads to more bus. risk. Small sales declines cause big profit declines.

Typical situation: can use operating leverage to get higher E(EBIT), but risk increases.

Copyright © 1996 by The Dryden Press. All rights reserved.

What is financial leverage? Financial risk?

- **Financial leverage:** Use of debt and pfd. stk.

- **Financial risk:** Additional risk placed on stockholders as a result of financial leverage.

Business Risk vs. Financial Risk

- **Business risk** depends on business factors such as competition, product liability, and operating leverage.

- **Financial risk** depends **only** on type of securities issued: More debt, more fin. risk.

Consider 2 hypothetical firms:

Firm U	Firm L
No Debt	$10,000 of 12% debt
$20,000 in assets	$20,000 in assets
40% tax rate	40% tax rate

Both firms have same op. leverage, business risk, prob. distr. of EBIT. Differ only W.R.T. financing used (cap. structure).

Copyright © 1996 by The Dryden Press. All rights reserved.

Firm U: Unleveraged	Economy		
	Bad	**Avg.**	**Good**
Prob.	0.25	0.50	0.25
Sales	$6,000	$9,000	$12,000
Op. costs	4,000	6,000	8,000
EBIT	$2,000	$3,000	$ 4,000
Interest	0	0	0
EBT	$2,000	$3,000	$ 4,000
Taxes (40%)	800	1,200	1,600
NI	$1,200	$1,800	$ 2,400

Firm L: Leveraged	Economy		
	Bad	**Avg.**	**Good**
Prob.*	0.25	0.50	0.25
Sales*	$6,000	$9,000	$12,000
Op. costs*	4,000	6,000	8,000
EBIT*	$2,000	$3,000	$ 4,000
INT (12%)	1,200	1,200	1,200
EBT	$ 800	$1,800	$ 2,800
Taxes (40%)	320	720	1,120
NI	$ 480	$1,080	$ 1,680

*Same as for Firm U.

Firm U	Bad	Avg.	Good
BEP*	10.0%	15.0%	20.0%
ROE	6.0%	9.0%	12.0%
TIE	∞	∞	∞

Firm L	Bad	Avg.	Good
BEP*	10.0%	15.0%	20.0%
ROE	4.8%	10.8%	16.8%
TIE	1.7x	2.5x	3.3x

*Same for U and L.

BLUEPRINTS: CHAPTER 12

Copyright © 1996 by The Dryden Press. All rights reserved.

Expected Values:	U	L
E(BEP)	15.0%	15.0%
E(ROE)	9.0%	10.8%
E(TIE)	∞	2.5x
Risk:		
σ_{ROE}	2.12%	4.24%
CV_{ROE}	0.24%	0.39%

Conclusions:

- Basic earning power = BEP = EBIT/Total assets: Unaffected by financial leverage.

- L has higher expected ROI and ROE because of tax savings.

- L has much wider ROE (and EPS) swings because of fixed interest charges.

- For leverage to raise expected ROE, must have BEP > k_d.

- **Why?** If k_d > BEP, then the interest expense will be higher than the operating income produced by debt-financed assets, so leverage will depress income.

Copyright © 1996 by The Dryden Press. All rights reserved.

If debt increases, TIE falls.

$$TIE = \frac{EBIT}{I}.$$

EBIT is constant (unaffected by use of debt), and since I = k_d D, as D increases, TIE must fall.

Optimal Capital Structure:

That capital structure (mix of debt, pfd, and common equity) at which P_0 is maximized. Trades off higher E(ROE) and EPS against higher risk.

What are "signaling" effects in capital structure?

Assumptions:

- **Managers have better info. about a firm's long-run value than outside investors.**

- **Managers act in the best interests of current stockholders.**

Copyright © 1996 by The Dryden Press. All rights reserved.

Therefore, managers can be expected to:

- issue stock if they think stock is overvalued.

- issue debt if they think stock is undervalued.

As a result, investors view a common stock offering as a negative signal -- managers think stock is overvalued.

Estimated costs of debt and equity for Campus Deli (see p. 1):

Amt borrowed	k_d	k_s
$ 0	10.0%	15.0%
250	10.0	15.5
500	11.0	16.5
750	13.0	18.0
1,000	16.0	20.0

Describe the sequence of events in a recapitalization.

- Campus Deli announces the recapitalization.

- New debt is issued.

- Proceeds are used to repurchase stock.

- Shares bought $= \dfrac{\text{Debt issued}}{\text{Price per share}}$

Copyright © 1996 by The Dryden Press. All rights reserved.

12-22

What would the new stock price be if Campus Deli recapitalized and used these amounts of debt: $0, $250,000, $500,000, $750,000? Assume EBIT = $500,000, T = 40%, and shares can be repurchased at $P_0 = \$20$.

D = 0:

$$EPS_0 = \frac{(EBIT - k_d D)(1 - T)}{\text{Shares outstanding}}$$

$$= \frac{\$500,000(0.6)}{100,000} = \$3.00.$$

12-23

D = $250, k_d = 10%.

$$\text{Shares repurchased} = \frac{\$250,000}{\$20} = 12,500.$$

$$EPS_1 = \frac{[\$500 - 0.1(\$250)](0.6)}{100 - 12.5}$$

$$= \$3.26.$$

$$TIE = \frac{EBIT}{I} = \frac{500}{25} = 20x.$$

12-24

D = $500, k_d = 11%.

$$\text{Shares repurchased} = \frac{\$500}{\$20} = 25.$$

$$EPS_2 = \frac{[\$500 - 0.11(\$500)](0.6)}{100 - 25}$$

$$= \$3.56.$$

$$TIE = \frac{EBIT}{I} = \frac{\$500}{\$55} = 9.1x.$$

Copyright © 1996 by The Dryden Press. All rights reserved.

Stock Price (zero growth):

$$P_0 = \frac{D_1}{k_s - g} = \frac{EPS}{k_s} = \frac{DPS}{k_s}$$

If payout = 100%, then EPS = DPS and E(g) = 0.

We just calculated EPS = DPS, and k_s was given on Page 1, so we can use the equation to find P_0 as shown on next slide.

$P_0 = DPS/k_s$:

Debt	DPS	k_s	P_0
$ 0	$3.00	15.0%	$20.00
250,000	3.26	15.5	21.03
500,000	3.56	16.5	21.58*
750,000	3.86	18.0	21.44
1,000,000	4.08	20.0	20.40

*Maximum: Since D = $500,000 and assets = $2,000,000, optimal D/A = 25%.

What debt ratio maximizes EPS?

See preceding slide. Max. EPS = $4.08 at

D = $1,000,000, and D/A = 50%.

Risk is too high at D/A = 50%.

Copyright © 1996 by The Dryden Press. All rights reserved.

What is Campus Deli's Optimal Capital Structure?

P_0 is maximized ($21.58) at D/A = 500,000/2,000,000 = 25%, so optimal D/A = 25%.

EPS is max. at 50%, but primary interest is stock price, not E(EPS).

The example shows that we can push up E(EPS) by using more debt, but the risk resulting from increased leverage more than offsets the benefit of higher E(EPS).

What's WACC at D = 0, D = $500, D = $1,000?

$$WACC = w_d k_d (1 - T) + w_{ce} k_e$$

D = 0:
WACC =   0   + 1.0(15%) = 15.0%.

D = 500:
WACC = .25(11)(.6) + .75(16.5) = 14.0%.

D = 1,000:
WACC = .50(16)(.6) + .50(20.0) = 14.8%.

Copyright © 1996 by The Dryden Press. All rights reserved.

12-31

12-32

DOL =

$$\frac{\%\Delta\ EBIT}{\%\Delta\ Sales} = \frac{S-VC}{S-VC-F} = \frac{S-VC}{EBIT}.$$

Given: S = $1,350; VC = 0.6; F = $40

$$DOL = \frac{1,350 - .6(1,350)}{1,350 - .6(1,350) - 40} = 1.08x$$

Therefore, EBIT increases 8% faster than sales due to operating leverage. DOL would be different at any different base sales level.

12-33

DFL =

$$\frac{\%\Delta\ NI\ (or\ EPS)}{\%\Delta\ EBIT} = \frac{EBIT}{EBIT-I} = \frac{S-VC-F}{S-VC-F-I}$$

At D = $500 and k_d = 11%

$$DFL = \frac{1,350 - .6(1,350) - 40}{1,350 - .6(1,350) - 40 - .11(500)}$$

$$= \frac{500}{445} = 1.1236.$$

NI (and EPS) increases 12.36% faster than EBIT due to financial leverage.

Copyright © 1996 by The Dryden Press. All rights reserved.

$$DTL = \frac{\%\Delta EPS}{\%\Delta S}$$

$$= (DOL)(DFL) = (1.08)(1.1236)$$
$$= 1.2135x.$$

Therefore, a 10% sales increase would cause a 10%(1.2135) = 12.13% increase in NI and EPS:

$$\%\Delta EPS = 1.2135(\%\Delta S).$$

EPS increases 21.35% faster than sales due to DOL and DFL.

Example:

Assume:

D = \$500; S_1 = \$1,350; VC = 0.6;
F = 40; N = 75,000 shares outstanding.

$$EPS_1 = \frac{[1,350 - .6(1,350) - 40 - .11(500)](.6)}{75}$$

$$= \frac{267}{75} = \$3.56.$$

Now sales rise by 10% to \$1,485:

$$EPS_2 = \frac{[1,485 - .6(1,485) - 40 - .11(500)](.6)}{75}$$

$$= 299.40 / 75 = \$3.99.$$

$$\%\Delta EPS = \frac{3.99 - 3.56}{3.56} = 12.1\%.$$

A 10% sales increase led to a 12.1% increase in EPS. That's 21% larger than the sales increase.

Copyright © 1996 by The Dryden Press. All rights reserved.

Conclusions on Degree of Leverage:

1. The higher the op. leverage, the more sensitive EBIT and EPS will be to changing sales.

2. Financial leverage amplifies the effects of changing sales on EPS.

3. High DOL and DFL can combine to lead to very high DTL, hence to very volatile EPS.

How Would These Factors Affect the Target Capital Structure?

1. Sales stability?
2. High operating leverage?
3. Increase in the corporate tax rate?
4. Increase in the personal tax rate?
5. Increase in bankruptcy costs?
6. Management spending lots of money on lavish perks?

- The graph shows MM's tax benefit vs. bankruptcy cost theory.
- Logical, but doesn't tell whole capital structure story. Main problem—assumes investors have same info. as managers.

Copyright © 1996 by The Dryden Press. All rights reserved.

Signaling theory, discussed earlier, suggests firms should use less debt than MM suggest.

This **unused debt capacity** helps avoid stock sales, which depress P_0 because of signaling effects.

Conclusions on Capital Structure:

1. Need to make calculations as we did, but should also recognize inputs are "guesstimates."

2. As a result of imprecise numbers, capital structure decisions have a large judgmental content.

3. We end up with capital structures varying widely among firms, even similar ones in same industry.

Copyright © 1996 by The Dryden Press. All rights reserved.

EXAM-TYPE PROBLEMS

1. If a firm uses debt financing (debt ratio = 0.4) and sales change from the current level, which of the following statements is most correct?

   a. The percentage change in net operating income (EBIT) resulting from the change in sales will exceed the percentage change in net income.

   b. The percentage change in EBIT will equal the percentage change in net income.

   c. The percentage change in net income relative to the percentage change in sales (and in EBIT) will not depend on the interest rate paid on the debt.

   d. The percentage change in net operating income will be less than the percentage change in net income.

   e. Since debt is used, the degree of operating leverage must be greater than 1.

2. If you know that your firm is facing relatively poor prospects but needs new capital, and you know that investors do not have this information, signalling theory would predict that you would

   a. Issue debt to maintain the returns of equity holders.

   b. Issue equity to share the burden of decreased equity returns between old and new shareholders.

   c. Be indifferent between issuing debt and equity.

   d. Postpone going into capital markets until your firm's prospects improve.

   e. Convey your inside information to investors using the media to eliminate the information asymmetry.

3. Howell Enterprises is forecasting EPS of $4.00 per share for next year. The firm has 10,000 shares outstanding, it pays 12% interest on its debt, and it faces a 40% marginal tax rate. Its estimated fixed costs are $80,000 while its variable costs are estimated at 40% of revenue. The firm's target capital structure is 40% equity and 60% debt and it has total assets of $400,000. On what level of sales is Howell basing its EPS forecast?

4. A company currently sells 75,000 units annually. At this sales level, its EBIT is $4 million, and its degree of total leverage is 2.0. The firm's debt consists of $15 million in bonds with a 9.5 percent coupon. The company is considering a new production method which will entail an increase in fixed costs, resulting in a degree of operating leverage of 1.6. Being concerned about the total risk of the firm, the president wants to keep the degree of total leverage at 2.0. If EBIT remains at $4 million, what amount of bonds must be retired to accomplish this?

Copyright © 1996 by The Dryden Press. All rights reserved.

13-8 Southeastern Steel Company (SSC) was formed 5 years ago to exploit a new continuous-casting process. SSC's founders, Donald Brown and Margo Valencia, had been employed in the research department of a major integrated-steel company, but when that company decided against using the new process (which Brown and Valencia had developed), they decided to strike out on their own. One advantage of the new process was that it required relatively little capital in comparison with the typical steel company, so Brown and Valencia have been able to avoid issuing new stock, and thus they own all of the shares. However, SCC has now reached the stage where outside equity capital is necessary if the firm is to achieve its growth targets yet still maintain its target capital structure of 60 percent equity and 40 percent debt. Therefore, Brown and Valencia have decided to take the company public. Until now, Brown and Valencia have paid themselves reasonable salaries but routinely reinvested all after-tax earnings in the firm, so dividend policy has not been an issue. However, before talking with potential outside investors, they must decide on a dividend policy.

Assume that you were recently hired by Arthur Adamson & Company (AA), a national consulting firm, which has been asked to help SSC prepare for its public offering. Martha Millon, the senior AA consultant in your group, has asked you to make a presentation to Brown and Valencia in which you review the theory of dividend policy and discuss the following questions.

a. (1)   What is meant by the term "dividend policy"?

   (2)   The terms "irrelevance," "bird-in-the-hand," and "tax preference" have been used to describe three major theories regarding the way dividend policy affects a firm's value. Explain what these terms mean, and briefly describe each theory.

   (3)   What do the three theories indicate regarding the actions management should take with respect to dividend policy?

   (4)   Explain the relationships between dividend policy, stock price, and the cost of equity under each dividend policy theory by constructing two graphs such as those shown in Figure 13-1. Dividend payout should be placed on the X axis.

   (5)   What results have empirical studies of the dividend theories produced? How does all this affect what we can tell managers about dividend policy?

Copyright © 1996 by The Dryden Press. All rights reserved.

b. Discuss (1) the information content, or signaling, hypothesis, (2) the clientele effect, and (3) their effects on dividend policy.

c. (1) Assume that SSC has an $800,000 capital budget planned for the coming year. You have determined that its present capital structure (60 percent equity and 40 percent debt) is optimal, and its net income is forecasted at $600,000. Use the residual dividend policy approach to determine SSC's total dollar dividend and payout ratio. In the process, explain what the residual dividend policy is, and use a graph to illustrate your answer. Then, explain what would happen if net income were forecasted at $400,000, or at $800,000.

   (2) In general terms, how would a change in investment opportunities affect the payout ratio under the residual payment policy?

   (3) What are the advantages and disadvantages of the residual policy? (Hint: Don't neglect signaling and clientele effects.)

d. What are some other commonly used dividend payment policies? What are their advantages and disadvantages? Which policy is most widely used in practice?

e. What is a dividend reinvestment plan (DRP), and how does it work?

f. Describe the series of steps that most firms take in setting dividend policy in practice.

g. What are stock repurchases? Discuss the advantages and disadvantages of a firm's repurchasing its own shares.

h. What are stock dividends and stock splits? What are the advantages and disadvantages of stock dividends and stock splits?

Copyright © 1996 by The Dryden Press. All rights reserved.

CHAPTER 13
Dividend Policy

- Theories of Investor Preferences
- Signaling Effects
- Residual Model
- Dividend Reinvestment Plans
- Stock Repurchases
- Stock Dividends and Stock Splits

What is "dividend policy"?

- It's the decision to pay out earnings versus retaining and reinvesting them. Includes these elements:

1. High or low payout?
2. Stable or irregular dividends?
3. How frequent?
4. Do we announce the policy?

Do investors prefer high or low payouts? There are three theories:

- Dividends are irrelevant: Investors don't care about payout.

- Bird in the hand: Investors prefer a high payout.

- Tax preference: Investors prefer a low payout, hence growth.

Copyright © 1996 by The Dryden Press. All rights reserved.

Dividend Irrelevance Theory:

- Investors are indifferent between dividends and retention-generated capital gains. If they want cash, they can sell stock. If they don't want cash, they can use dividends to buy stock.

- Modigliani-Miller support irrelevance.

- Theory is based on unrealistic assumptions (no taxes or brokerage costs), hence may not be true. Need empirical test.

Bird-in-the-Hand Theory:

- Investors think dividends are less risky than potential future capital gains, hence they like dividends.

- If so, investors would value high payout firms more highly, i.e., a high payout would result in a high P_0.

Tax Preference Theory:

- Retained earnings lead to capital gains, which are taxed at lower rates than dividends: 28% max. vs. up to 39.6%. Capital gains taxes are also deferred.

- This could cause investors to prefer firms with low payouts, i.e., a high payout results in a low P_0.

Copyright © 1996 by The Dryden Press. All rights reserved.

Implications of 3 theories for managers:

Theory:	Implication:
Irrelevance	Any payout OK
Bird in the hand	Set high payout
Tax preference	Set low payout

But which, if any, is correct???

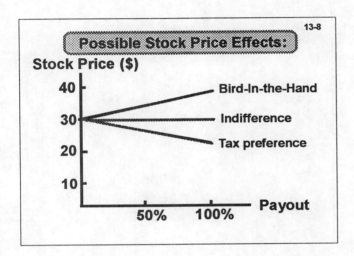

Possible Stock Price Effects:

Stock Price ($)

- Bird-In-the-Hand
- Indifference
- Tax preference

Payout

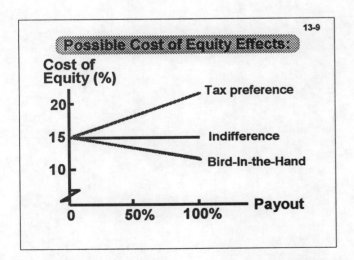

Possible Cost of Equity Effects:

Cost of Equity (%)

- Tax preference
- Indifference
- Bird-In-the-Hand

Payout

Copyright © 1996 by The Dryden Press. All rights reserved.

Which Theory is most Correct?

- Empirical testing has not been able to determine which theory, if any, is correct.

- Thus, managers must use judgment when setting policy.

- Analysis is used, but it must be applied with judgment.

What's the "information content", or "signaling", hypothesis?

- Managers hate to cut divs, so won't raise div. unless they think raise is sustainable. So, investors view dividend increases as signals of management's view of the future.

- Therefore, a stock price increase at time of dividend increase could reflect higher expectations for future EPS, not a desire for divs.

What's the "clientele effect"?

- Different groups of investors, or clienteles, prefer different dividend policies.

- Firm's past div. policy determines its current clientele of investors.

- Clientele effects impede changing dividend policy. Taxes & brokerage costs hurt investors who have to switch companies.

BLUEPRINTS: CHAPTER 13

Copyright © 1996 by The Dryden Press. All rights reserved.

What's the "residual dividend model"?

- Find the retained earnings needed for the capital budget.
- Pay out any leftover earnings (the residual) as dividends.
- This policy minimizes flotation and equity signaling costs, hence minimizes the WACC.

Blue = WACC$_1$
Red = WACC$_2$

Data for SSC:

- Capital budget: $800,000. Given.
- Target capital structure: 40% debt, 60% equity. Want to maintain.
- Forecasted net income: $600,000.
- How much of the $600,000 should we pay out as dividends?

Copyright © 1996 by The Dryden Press. All rights reserved.

Of the $800,000 capital budget, 0.6($800,000) = $480,000 must be equity to keep at target capital structure. [0.4($800,000) = $320,000 will be debt.]

With $600,000 of net income, the residual is $600,000 - $480,000 = $120,000 = dividends paid.

Payout ratio = $120,000/$600,000 = 0.20 = 20%.

How would a drop in NI to $400,000 affect the dividend? A rise to $800,000?

- NI = $400,000: Need $480,000 of equity, so should retain the whole $400,000. Divs = 0.
- NI = $800,000: Divs = $800,000 - $480,000 = $320,000. Payout = 320,000/800,000 = 40%.

How would a change in investment opportunities affect dividend under the residual policy?

- Fewer good investments would lead to smaller cap. bud., hence to a higher dividend payout.
- More good investments would lead to a lower dividend payout.

Copyright © 1996 by The Dryden Press. All rights reserved.

Advantages and disadvantages of the residual dividend policy.

- **Advantages:** Minimizes new stock issues and flotation costs.
- **Disadvantages:** Results in variable dividends, sends conflicting signals, increases risk, and doesn't appeal to any specific clientele.
- **Conclusion:** Consider residual policy when setting target payout, but don't follow it rigidly.

Alternative Dividend Policies

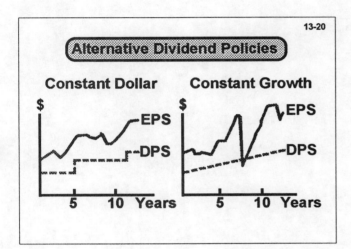

Constant Dollar

Constant Growth

What's a "dividend reinvestment plan (DRP)"?

- Shareholders can automatically reinvest their dividends in shares of the company's common stock. Get more stock rather than cash.
- There are two types of plans:
  (1) Open market
  (2) New stock

Copyright © 1996 by The Dryden Press. All rights reserved.

Open market purchase plan:

- Dollars to be reinvested are turned over to trustee, who buys shares on the open market.

- Brokerage costs are reduced by volume purchases.

- Convenient, easy way to invest, thus useful for investors.

New stock plan:

- Firm issues new stock to DRP enrollees, keeps money and uses it to buy assets.

- No fees are charged, plus sells stock at discount of 5% from market price, which is about equal to flotation costs of underwritten stock offering.

Optional investments sometimes possible, up to $150,000 or so.

Firms that need new equity capital use new stock plans.

Firms with no need for new equity capital use open market purchase plans.

Most NYSE listed companies have a DRP. Useful for investors.

Copyright © 1996 by The Dryden Press. All rights reserved.

Setting Dividend Policy.

- Forecast capital needs over a planning horizon, often 5 years.
- Set a target capital structure.
- Estimate annual equity needs.
- Set target payout based on the residual model.
- Generally, some div. growth rate emerges. Maintain target growth rate if possible, varying capital structure somewhat if necessary.

Stock repurchases:

Repurchases: Buying own stock back from stockholders.

Reasons for repurchases:

- As an alternative to distributing cash as dividends.

- To dispose of one-time cash from an asset sale.

- To make a large capital structure change.

Advantages of repurchases:

- Stockholders can tender or not.
- Helps avoid setting a high dividend that cannot be maintained.
- Repurchased stock can be used in takeovers or resold to raise cash as needed.
- Income received is capital gains rather than higher-taxed dividends.
- Stockholders may take as a positive signal--mgt. thinks stock undervalued.

Copyright © 1996 by The Dryden Press. All rights reserved.

Disadvantages of repurchases:

- May be viewed as a negative signal (firm has poor investment opp.).
- IRS could impose penalties if repurchases were primarily to avoid taxes on dividends.
- Selling stockholders may not be well informed, hence be treated unfairly.
- Firm may have to bid up price to complete repurchase, thus paying too much for its own stock.

Stock Dividends vs. Stock Splits:

- **Stock dividend:** Firm issues new shares in lieu of paying a cash dividend. If 10%, get 10 shares for each 100 owned.
- **Stock split:** Firm increases the number of shares outstanding, say 2:1. Sends shareholders more shares.

Both stock dividends and stock splits increase the number of shares outstanding, so "the pie is divided into smaller pieces".

Unless the stock dividend or split conveys information, or is accompanied by another event like higher dividends, the stock price falls so as to keep each investor's wealth unchanged.

But splits/stock dividends may get us to an "optimal price range".

Copyright © 1996 by The Dryden Press. All rights reserved.

When should a firm consider splitting its stock?

- There's a widespread belief that the **optimal price range** for stocks is $20 to $80.
- Stock splits can be used to keep the price in the optimal range.
- Stock splits generally occur when mgt. is confident, so are interpreted as **positive signals**.

Copyright © 1996 by The Dryden Press. All rights reserved.

EXAM-TYPE PROBLEMS

1. If you were to argue that the firm's cost of equity, k_s, increases as the dividend payout decreases, you would be making an argument _____ with MM's dividend irrelevance theory, and _____ with Gordon and Lintner's "bird-in-the-hand" theory.

   a. consistent; consistent

   b. inconsistent; consistent

   c. consistent; inconsistent

   d. inconsistent; inconsistent

   e. The argument above does not make sense, neither theory involves the cost of equity capital.

2. Which of the following statements is most correct?

   a. If the *dividend irrelevance theory* (which is associated with the names Modigliani and Miller) were exactly correct, and if this theory could be tested with "clean" data, then we would find, in a regression of dividend yield and capital gains, a line with a slope of -1.0.

   b. The *tax preference* and *bird-in-the-hand* theories lead to identical conclusions as to the optimal dividend policy.

   c. If a company raises its dividend by an unexpectedly large amount, the announcement of this new and higher dividend is generally accompanied by an increase in the stock price. This is consistent with the bird-in-the-hand theory, and Modigliani and Miller used these findings to support their position on dividend theory.

   d. If it could be demonstrated that a *clientele effect* exists, this would suggest that firms could alter their dividend payment policies from year to year to take advantage of investment opportunities without having to worry about the effects of changing dividends on capital costs.

   e. Each of the above statements is false.

3. Driver Corporation faces an investment opportunity schedule (IOS) calling for a capital budget of $60 million. Its optimal capital structure is 60% equity and 40% debt. Its earnings before interest and taxes (EBIT) were $98 million for the year. The firm has $200 million in assets, pays an average of 10% on all its debt, and faces a marginal tax rate of 34 percent. If the firm maintains a residual dividend policy and will finance its capital budget so as to keep its optimal capital structure intact, what will be the amount of the dividends it pays out?

Copyright © 1996 by The Dryden Press. All rights reserved.

14-8 Sue Wilson, the new financial manager of New World Chemicals (NWC), a California producer of specialized chemicals for use in fruit orchards, must prepare a financial forecast for 1996. NWC's 1995 sales were $2 billion, and the marketing department is forecasting a 25 percent increase for 1996. Wilson thinks the company was operating at full capacity in 1995, but she is not sure about this. The 1995 financial statements, plus some other data, are given in Table IC14-1.

Table IC14-1. Financial Statements and Other Data on NWC
(Millions of dollars)

A. 1995 Balance Sheet

Cash & securities	$ 20	Accounts payable and accruals	$ 100
Accounts receivable	240	Notes payable	100
Inventory	240	Total current liabilities	$ 200
Total current assets	$ 500	Long-term debt	100
Net fixed assets	500	Common stock	500
		Retained earnings	200
Total assets	$1,000	Total liabilities and equity	$1,000

B. 1995 Income Statement

Sales	$2,000.00
Less: Variable costs	1,200.00
Fixed costs	700.00
Earnings before interest and taxes	$ 100.00
Interest	16.00
Earnings before taxes	$ 84.00
Taxes (40%)	33.60
Net income	$ 50.40
Dividends (30%)	$ 15.12
Addition to retained earnings	$ 35.28

C. Key ratios

	NWC	Industry	Comment
Basic earnings power	10.00%	20.00%	
Profit margin	2.52%	4.00%	
Return on equity	7.20%	15.60%	
Days sales outstanding (360 days)	43.20 days	32.00 days	
Inventory turnover	8.33×	11.00×	
Fixed assets turnover	4.00×	5.00×	
Total assets turnover	2.00×	2.50×	
Debt/assets	30.00%	36.00%	
Times interest earned	6.25×	9.40×	
Current ratio	2.50×	3.00×	
Payout ratio	30.00%	30.00%	

Copyright © 1996 by The Dryden Press. All rights reserved.

Assume that you were recently hired as Wilson's assistant, and your first major task is to help her develop the forecast. She asked you to begin by answering the following set of questions.

a. Assume (1) that NWC was operating at full capacity in 1995 with respect to all assets, (2) that all assets must grow proportionally with sales, (3) that accounts payable and accruals will also grow in proportion to sales, and (4) that the 1995 profit margin and dividend payout will be maintained. Under these conditions, what will the company's financial requirements be for the coming year? Use the AFN equation to answer this question.

b. Now estimate the 1996 financial requirements using the projected financial statement approach, making an initial ("first pass") forecast plus one additional "pass" to determine the effects of "financing feedbacks." Assume (1) that each type of asset, as well as payables, accruals, and fixed and variable costs, grow at the same rate as sales; (2) that the payout ratio is held constant at 30 percent; (3) that external funds needed are financed 50 percent by notes payable and 50 percent by long-term debt (no new common stock will be issued); and (4) that all debt carries an interest rate of 8 percent.

c. Why do the two methods produce somewhat different AFN forecasts? Which method provides the more accurate forecast?

d. Calculate NWC's forecasted ratios, and compare them with the company's 1995 ratios and with the industry averages. How does NWC compare with the average firm in its industry, and is the company expected to improve during the coming year?

e. Suppose you now learn that NWC's 1995 receivables and inventory were in line with required levels, given the firm's credit and inventory policies, but that excess capacity existed with regard to fixed assets. Specifically, fixed assets were operated at only 75 percent of capacity.

   (1)   What level of sales could have existed in 1995 with the available fixed assets? What would the fixed assets/sales ratio have been if NWC had been operating at full capacity?

   (2)   How would the existence of excess capacity in fixed assets affect the additional funds needed during 1996?

f. Without actually working out the numbers, how would you expect the ratios to change in the situation where excess capacity in fixed assets exists? Explain your reasoning.

Copyright © 1996 by The Dryden Press. All rights reserved.

g. Based on comparisons between NWC's days sales outstanding (DSO) and inventory turnover ratios with the industry average figures, does it appear that NWC is operating efficiently with respect to its inventory and accounts receivable? If the company were able to bring these ratios into line with the industry averages, what effect would this have on its AFN and its financial ratios. (Note: Inventory and receivables will be discussed in detail in Chapter 15.)

h. The relationship between sales and the various types of assets is important in financial forecasting. The financial statement method, under the assumption that each asset item grows at the same rate as sales, leads to an AFN forecast that is reasonably close to the forecast using the AFN equation. Explain how each of the following factors would affect the accuracy of financial forecasts based on the AFN equation: (1) excess capacity, (2) base stocks of assets, such as shoes in a shoe store, (3) economies of scale in the use of assets, and (4) lumpy assets.

i. (1) How could regression analysis be used to detect the presence of the situations described above and then to improve the financial forecasts? Plot a graph of the following data, which is for a typical well-managed company in NWC's industry, to illustrate your answer.

	Sales	Inventories
1993	$1,280	$118
1994	1,600	138
1995	2,000	162
1996E	2,500	192

(2) On the same graph that plots the above data, draw a line which shows how the regression line would have to appear to justify the use of the AFN formula and the projected financial statement forecasting method. As a part of your answer, show the growth rate in inventory that results from a 10 percent increase in sales from a sales level of (a) $200 and (b) $2,000 based on both the actual regression line and a hypothetical regression line which is linear and which goes through the origin.

j. How would changes in these items affect the AFN? (1) The dividend payout ratio, (2) the profit margin, (3) the capital intensity ratio, and (4) if NWC begins buying from its suppliers on terms which permit it to pay after 60 days rather than after 30 days. (Consider each item separately and hold all other things constant.)

Copyright © 1996 by The Dryden Press. All rights reserved.

CHAPTER 14
Financial Forecasting

- **Forecast Sales**
- **Project the Assets Needed to Support Sales**
- **Project Internally Generated Funds**
- **Project Outside Funds Needed**
- **Decide How to Raise Funds**
- **See Effects of Plan on Ratios**

1995 Balance Sheet: (in millions of $)

Cash and sec.	$ 20	Accts. pay and accruals	$ 100
Accounts rec.	240	Notes payable	100
Inventories	240	Total CL	$ 200
Total CA	$ 500	L-T debt	100
		Common stock	500
Net fixed assets	500	Retained earnings	200
Total assets	$1,000	Total claims	$1,000

1995 Income Statement: (in millions of $)

Sales	$2,000.00
Less: Var. costs (60%)	1,200.00
Fixed costs	700.00
EBIT	$ 100.00
Interest	16.00
EBT	$ 84.00
Taxes (40%)	33.60
Net income	$ 50.40
Dividends (30%)	$ 15.12
Add'n to RE	$ 35.28

Copyright © 1996 by The Dryden Press. All rights reserved.

Key ratios:

	NWC	Industry	Condition
BEP	10.00%	20.00%	Poor
Profit margin	2.52%	4.00%	"
ROE	7.20%	15.60%	"
DSO	43.2 days	32.0 days	"
Inv. turnover	8.33x	11.00x	"
F. A. turnover	4.00x	5.00x	"
T. A. turnover	2.00x	2.50x	"
Debt/assets ratio	30.00%	36.00%	Good
TIE	6.25x	9.40x	Poor
Current ratio	2.50x	3.00x	"
Payout ratio	30.00%	30.00%	O.K.

Key Assumptions:

- Operating at full capacity in 1995.
- Each type of asset grows proportionally with sales.
- Payables and accruals grow proportionally with sales.
- 1995 profit margin (2.52%) and payout (30%) will be maintained.
- Sales are expected to increase by $500 million. (%ΔS = 25%)

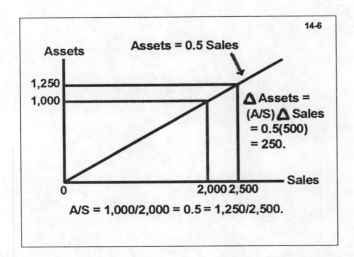

Assets = 0.5 Sales

Δ Assets = (A/S) Δ Sales = 0.5(500) = 250.

A/S = 1,000/2,000 = 0.5 = 1,250/2,500.

Copyright © 1996 by The Dryden Press. All rights reserved.

Assets must increase by $250 million. What is the AFN, based on the AFN equation?

$$AFN = (A^*/S)\Delta S - (L^*/S)\Delta S$$
$$- M(S_1)(1 - d)$$
$$= (\$1,000 / \$2,000)(\$500)$$
$$- (\$100 / \$2,000)(\$500)$$
$$- 0.0252(\$2,500)(1 - 0.3)$$
$$= \$180.9 \text{ million.}$$

Assumptions about how AFN will be raised:

- The payout ratio will remain at 30 percent (d = 30%).
- No new common stock will be issued.
- Any external funds needed will be raised as debt, 50% notes payable and 50% L-T debt. All new debt will cost 8 percent.

1996 1ˢᵗ Pass Income Statement:

	1995	Factor	1st Pass
Sales	$2,000	x1.25	$2,500
Less: VC	1,200	x1.25	1,500
FC	700	x1.25	875
EBIT	$ 100		$ 125
Interest	16	→	16
EBT	$ 84		$ 109
Taxes (40%)	34		44
Net income	$ 50		$ 65
Div. (30%)	$ 15		$ 19
Add. to RE	$ 35		$ 46

BLUEPRINTS: CHAPTER 14

Copyright © 1996 by The Dryden Press. All rights reserved.

1996 1st Pass Balance Sheet (Assets):

	1995	Factor	1st Pass
Cash/sec.	$ 20	x1.25	$ 25
Accts. rec.	240	x1.25	300
Inventories	240	x1.25	300
Total CA	$ 500		$ 625
Net FA	500	x1.25	625
Total assets	$ 1,000		$1,250

At full capacity, so all assets must increase in proportion to sales.

1996 1st Pass Balance Sheet (Claims):

	1995	Factor	1st Pass
AP/accruals	$ 100	x1.25	$ 125
Notes payable	100	→	100
Total CL	$ 200		$ 225
L-T debt	100	→	100
Common stk.	500	→	500
Ret. earnings	200	+ 46*	246
Total claims	$ 1,000		$1,071

*From 1st pass income statement.

What is the additional financing needed (AFN) after the first pass?

- Forecasted total assets = $1,250
- Forecasted total claims = $1,071
- Forecasted AFN$_1$ = $ 179

NWC must have the assets to make forecasted sales. The balance sheet must balance. So, we must raise $179 externally.

Copyright © 1996 by The Dryden Press. All rights reserved.

How will the AFN be financed?

Additional notes payable =
  0.5($179) = $89.50

Additional L-T debt =
  0.5($179) = $89.50

But this financing will add
0.08($179) = $14.32 to interest
expense, which will lower NI and
retained earnings.

1996 2nd Pass Income Statement:

	1st Pass	Fdbk.	2nd Pass
Sales	$2,500	→	$2,500
Less: VC	1,500	→	1,500
FC	875	→	875
EBIT	$ 125	→	$ 125
Interest	16	+14	30
EBT	$ 109		$ 95
Taxes (40%)	44		38
Net income	$ 65		$ 57
Div. (30%)	$ 19		$ 17
Add. to RE	$ 46		$ 40

1996 2nd Pass Balance Sheet (Assets):

	1st Pass	Fdbk.	2nd Pass
Cash/sec.	$ 25	→	$ 25
Accts. rec.	300	→	300
Inventories	300	→	300
Total CA	$ 625	→	$ 625
Net FA	625	→	625
Total assets	$ 1,250	→	$1,250

No change in asset requirements.

Copyright © 1996 by The Dryden Press. All rights reserved.

1996 2ⁿᵈ Pass Balance Sheet (Claims):

	1st Pass	Fdbk.	2nd Pass
AP/accruals	$ 125	⟶	$ 125
Notes payable	100	+89.5	190
Total CL	$ 225		$ 315
L-T debt	100	+89.5	189
Common stk.	500	⟶	500
Ret. earnings	246	-6	240
Total claims	$ 1,071		$1,244

Results after the second pass:

· **Forecasted assets = $1,250 (no change)**

· **Forecasted claims = $1,244 (higher)**

· **2nd pass AFN = $ 6 (short)**

· **Cumulative AFN = $179 + $6 = $185.**

· **The $6 shortfall came from reduced net earnings. Additional passes could be made until assets exactly equal claims. $6(0.08) = $0.48 interest 3rd pass.**

Equation AFN = $181 vs. $185. Why different?

· **Equation method assumes a constant profit margin.**

· **Financial statement method is more flexible. More important, it allows different items to grow at different rates.**

Copyright © 1996 by The Dryden Press. All rights reserved.

Ratios after 2nd pass:

	1995	1996(E)	Industry	
BEP	10.00%	10.00%	20.00%	Poor
Profit margin	2.52%	2.27%	4.00%	"
ROE	7.20%	7.68%	15.60%	"
DSO (days)	43.2	43.2	32.0	"
Inv. turnover	8.33x	8.33x	11.00x	"
FA turnover	4.00x	4.00x	5.00x	"
TA turnover	2.00x	2.00x	2.50x	"
D/A ratio	30.00%	40.34%	36.00%	"
TIE	6.25x	4.12%	9.40x	"
Current ratio	2.50x	1.99x	3.00x	"
Payout	30%	30%	30%	o.k.

Suppose in 1995 fixed assets had been operated at only 75% of capacity:

$$\frac{\text{Capacity}}{\text{sales}} = \frac{\text{Actual sales}}{\% \text{ of capacity}}$$

$$= \frac{\$2,000}{0.75} = \$2,667.$$

With the existing fixed assets, sales could be $2,667. Since sales are forecasted at only $2,500, no new fixed assets are needed.

How would the excess capacity situation affect the 1996 AFN?

- The projected increase in fixed assets was $125, the AFN would decrease by $125.

- Since no new fixed assets will be needed, AFN will fall by $125, to

$$\$185 - \$125 = \$60.$$

Copyright © 1996 by The Dryden Press. All rights reserved.

Q. If sales went up to $3,000, not $2,500, what would the F.A. requirement be?

A. Target ratio = FA/Capacity sales
$$= 500/2,667 = 18.75\%.$$

Have enough F.A. for sales up to $2,667, but need F.A. for another $333 of sales:

$$\Delta FA = 0.1875(333) = \$62.4.$$

How would excess capacity affect the forecasted ratios:

1. Sales wouldn't change but assets would be lower, so turnovers would be better.

2. Less new debt, hence lower interest, so higher profits, EPS, ROE.

3. Debt ratio, TIE would improve.

1996 Forecasted Ratios:

	% of Capacity in 1995:		
	100%	75%	Industry
BEP	10.00%	11.11%	20.00%
Profit margin	2.27%	2.51%	4.00%
ROE	7.68%	8.44%	15.60%
DSO (days)	43.2	43.2	32.0
Inv. turnover	8.33x	8.33x	11.00x
FA turnover	4.00x	5.00x	5.00x
TA turnover	2.00x	2.22x	2.50x
D/A ratio	40.34%	33.71%	36.00%
TIE	4.12%	6.15x	9.40x
Current ratio	1.99x	2.48x	3.00x

BLUEPRINTS: CHAPTER 14

Copyright © 1996 by The Dryden Press. All rights reserved.

How is NWC performing with regard to its receivables and inventories?

- DSO is higher than the industry average, and inventory turnover is lower than the industry average.

- Improvements here would lower current assets, reduce capital requirements, and further improve profitability and other ratios.

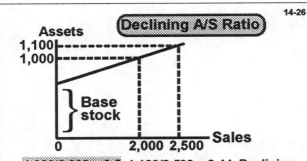

Declining A/S Ratio

1,000/2,000 = 0.5; 1,100/2,500 = 0.44. Declining ratio shows economies of scale. Going from S=0 to S=2,000 requires 1,000 of assets. Next 500 of sales requires only 100 of assets.

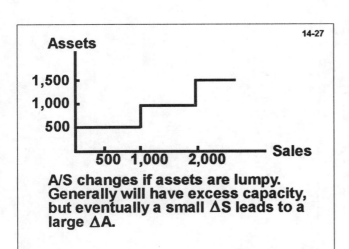

A/S changes if assets are lumpy. Generally will have excess capacity, but eventually a small ΔS leads to a large ΔA.

Copyright © 1996 by The Dryden Press. All rights reserved.

Summary: How different factors affect the AFN forecast.

- **Excess capacity:** Existence lowers AFN.
- **Base stocks of assets:** Leads to less-than-proportional asset increases.
- **Economies of scale:** Also leads to less-than-proportional asset increases.
- **Lumpy assets:** Leads to large periodic AFN requirements, recurring excess capacity.

Regression Analysis for Asset Forecasting

- Get historical data on a good company, then fit a regression line to see how much a given sales increase will require in way of asset increase.

Example of Regression:

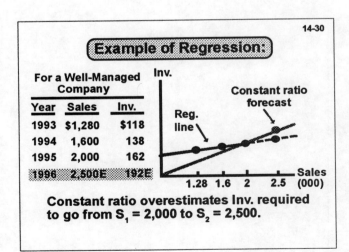

For a Well-Managed Company

Year	Sales	Inv.
1993	$1,280	$118
1994	1,600	138
1995	2,000	162
1996	2,500E	192E

Constant ratio overestimates Inv. required to go from $S_1 = 2,000$ to $S_2 = 2,500$.

Copyright © 1996 by The Dryden Press. All rights reserved.

Regression with 10B for our example:

- **Same as finding beta coefficients.**
- **Clear all**

  1280 Input   118 Σ^+
  1600 Input   138 Σ^+
  2000 Input   162 Σ^+

0 ■ ŷ,m → 40.0 = Inventory at sales = 0.
■ SWAP → 0.0611 = Slope coefficient.
Inventory = 40.0 + 0.0611 Sales.

LEAVE CALCULATOR ALONE!

Equation is now in the calculator. Let's use it by inputting new sales of $2,500 and getting forecasted inventory:

2500 ■ ŷ,m → 192.66.

The constant ratio forecast was Inventory = 300, so the regression forecast is lower by $107. This would free up $107 for use elsewhere, which would improve profitability and raise P_0.

How would increases in these items affect the AFN?

- **Higher dividend payout ratio?** Increase AFN: Less retained earnings.
- **Higher profit margin?** Decrease AFN: Higher profits, more retained earnings.
- **Higher capital intensity ratio, A/S?** Increase AFN: Need more assets for given sales increase.
- **Pay suppliers in 60 days rather than 30 days?** Decrease AFN, because trade creditors supply more capital, i.e., L*/S increases.

BLUEPRINTS: CHAPTER 14

Copyright © 1996 by The Dryden Press. All rights reserved.

EXAM-TYPE PROBLEMS

1. Snowball & Company has the following balance sheet:

Current assets	$ 7,000	A/P & Accruals	$ 1,500
Fixed assets	3,000	S-T (3 month) Loans	2,000
		Common Stock	1,500
		Ret. Earnings	5,000
Total Assets	$10,000	Total Claims	$10,000

Snowball's after-tax profit margin is 11%, and the company pays out 60 percent of its earnings as dividends. Its sales last year were $10,000; its assets were used to full capacity; no economies of scale exist in the use of assets; and the profit margin and payout ratio are expected to remain constant. The company uses the AFN equation to estimate funds requirements, and it plans to raise any required external capital as short-term bank loans. If sales grow by 50 percent, what will Snowball's current ratio be after it has raised the necessary expansion funds?

2. Hogan Inc. generated EBIT of $240,000 this past year using assets of $1,100,000. The interest rate on its existing long-term debt of $640,000 is 12.5 percent and the firm's tax rate is 40 percent. The firm paid a dividend of $1.27 on each of its 37,800 shares outstanding from net income of $96,000. The total book value of equity is $446,364 of which the common stock account equals $335,000. The firm's shares sell for $28.00 per share in the market. The firm forecasts a 10% increase in sales, assets, and EBIT next year, and a dividend of $1.40 per share. If the firm needs additional capital funds, it will raise 60% with debt and 40% with equity. The cost of any new debt will be 13%. Spontaneous liabilities are estimated at $15,000 for next year, representing an increase of 10% over this year. Except for spontaneous liabilities, the firm uses no other sources of current liabilities and will continue this policy in the future. What will be the cumulative AFN Hogan will need to balance its projected balance sheet using the projected balance sheet method through the first two passes?

3. Which of the following statements is most correct?

a. If the capital intensity ratio is high, this permits sales to grow more rapidly without much outside capital.

b. The lower the profit margin, the lower the additional funds needed because less assets are needed to support existing sales.

Copyright © 1996 by The Dryden Press. All rights reserved.

c. When positive economies of scale are present, linear balance sheet relationships no longer hold. As sales increase, a proportionately greater stock of assets is required to support the higher sales level.

d. Technological considerations often require firms to add fixed assets in large, discrete units. Such assets are called lumpy assets and they affect the firm's financial requirements through the fixed assets/sales ratio at different sales levels.

e. The projected balance sheet method accounts for changing balance sheet ratios and thus, cyclical changes in the actual sales/assets ratio do not have an impact on financing requirements.

Copyright © 1996 by The Dryden Press. All rights reserved.

15-8 Dan Barnes, financial manager of Ski Equipment Inc. (SKI), is excited but apprehensive. The company's founder recently sold his 51 percent controlling block of stock to Kent Koren, who is a big fan of EVA (Economic Value Added). EVA is found by taking the after-tax operating profit and then subtracting the dollar cost of all the capital the firm uses:

EVA = Sales revenues - Operating costs - Taxes - Capital costs
    = Sales - Operating costs - Taxes - WACC (Capital employed).

If EVA is positive, then the firm is creating value. On the other hand, if EVA is negative, the firm is not covering its cost of capital, and stockholders' value is being eroded. Koren rewards managers handsomely if they create value, but those whose operations produce negative EVAs are soon looking for work. Koren frequently points out that if a company can generate its current level of sales with less assets, it would need less capital. That would, other things held constant, lower capital costs and increase its EVA.

Shortly after he took control of SKI, Kent Koren met with SKI's senior executives to tell them of his plans for the company. First, he presented some EVA data which convinced everyone that SKI has not been creating value in recent years. He then stated, in no uncertain terms, that this situation must change. He noted that SKI's designs of skis, boots, and clothing are acclaimed throughout the industry, but something is seriously amiss elsewhere in the company. Costs are too high, prices are too low, the company employs too much capital, and he wants SKI's managers to correct the problem or else.

Barnes has long felt that SKI's working capital situation should be studied--the company may have the optimal amounts of cash, securities, receivables, and inventories, but it may also have too much or too little of these items. In the past, the production manager has resisted Dan's efforts to question his holdings of raw materials inventories, the marketing manager has resisted questions about finished goods, the sales staff has resisted questions about credit policy (which affects accounts receivable), and the treasurer has not wanted to talk about her cash and securities balances. Koren's speech made it clear that such resistance would no longer be tolerated.

Dan also knows that decisions about working capital cannot be made in a vacuum. For example, if inventories could be lowered without adversely affecting

Copyright © 1996 by The Dryden Press. All rights reserved.

operations, then less capital would be required, the dollar cost of capital would decline, and EVA would increase. However, lower raw materials inventories might lead to production slowdowns and higher costs, while lower finished goods inventories might lead to the loss of profitable sales. So, before inventories are changed, it will be necessary to study operating as well as financial effects. The situation is the same with regard to cash and receivables.

a. Dan plans to use the ratios in Table IC15-1 as the starting point for discussions with SKI's operating executives. He wants everyone to think about the pros and cons of changing each type of current asset and how changes would interact to affect profits and EVA. Based on the Table IC15-1 data, does SKI seem to be following a conservative, moderate, or aggressive working capital policy?

Table IC15-1. Selected Ratios: SKI and Industry Average

	SKI	Industry
Current	1.75x	2.25x
Quick	0.83x	1.20x
Debt/assets	58.76%	50.00%
Turnover of cash and securities	16.67x	22.22x
Days sales outstanding	45.00	32.00
Inventory turnover	4.82x	7.00x
Fixed assets turnover	11.35x	12.00x
Total assets turnover	2.08x	3.00x
Profit margin on sales	2.07%	3.50%
Return on equity (ROE)	10.45%	21.00%

b. How can one distinguish between a conservative but rational working capital policy and a situation where a firm simply has a lot of current assets because it is inefficient? Does SKI's working capital policy seem appropriate?

c. What might SKI do to reduce its cash and securities without harming operations?

d. What is "float," and how is it affected by the firm's cash manager (treasurer)?

In an attempt to better understand SKI's cash position, Dan developed a cash budget. Data for the first two months of the year are shown in Table IC15-2. (Note that Dan's preliminary cash budget does not account for interest income or interest expense.) He has the figures for the other months, but they are not shown in Table IC15-2.

Copyright © 1996 by The Dryden Press. All rights reserved.

Table IC15-2. SKI's Cash Budget for January and February

		NOV	DEC	JAN	FEB	MAR	APR
I. COLLECTIONS AND PURCHASES WORKSHEET							
(1)	Sales (gross)	$71,218	$68,212.00	$65,213.00	$52,475.00	$42,909	$30,524
Collections:							
(2)	During month of sale (0.2)(0.98)(month's sales)			12,781.75	10,285.10		
(3)	During first month after sale 0.7(previous month's sales)			47,748.40	45,649.10		
(4)	During second month after sale 0.1(sales 2 months ago)			7,121.80	6,821.20		
(5)	Total collections (Lines 2+3+4)			$67,651.95	$62,755.40		
Purchases:							
(6)	0.85(forecasted sales 2 months from now)		$44,603.75	$36,472.65	$25,945.40		
(7)	Payments (1-month lag)			44,603.75	36,472.65		
II. CASH GAIN OR LOSS FOR MONTH							
(8)	Collections (from Section I)			$67,651.95	$62,755.40		
(9)	Payments for purchases (from Section I)			44,603.75	36,472.65		
(10)	Wages and salaries			6,690.56	5,470.90		
(11)	Rent			2,500.00	2,500.00		
(12)	Taxes						
(13)	Total payments			$53,794.31	$44,443.55		
(14)	Net cash gain (loss) during month (Line 8 - Line 13)			$13,857.64	$18,311.85		
III. CASH SURPLUS OR LOAN REQUIREMENT							
(15)	Cash at beginning of month if no borrowing is done			$ 3,000.00	$16,857.64		
(16)	Cumulative cash (cash at start, + gain or - loss = Line 14 + Line 15)			16,857.64	35,169.49		
(17)	Target cash balance			1,500.00	1,500.00		
(18)	Cumulative surplus cash or loans outstanding to maintain $1,500 target cash balance (Line 16 - Line 17)			$15,357.64	$33,669.49		

e. Should depreciation expense be explicitly included in the cash budget? Why or why not?

f. In his preliminary cash budget, Dan has assumed that all sales are collected and, thus, that SKI has no bad debts. Is this realistic? If not, how would bad debts be dealt with in a cash budgeting sense? (Hint: Bad debts will affect collections but not purchases.)

g. Dan's cash budget for the entire year, although not given here, is based heavily on his forecast for monthly sales. Sales are expected to be extremely low between May and September but then to increase dramatically in the fall and winter. November is typically the firm's best month, when SKI ships equipment to retailers for the holiday season. Interestingly, Dan's forecasted cash budget indicates that the company's cash

---

BLUEPRINTS: CHAPTER 15

Copyright © 1996 by The Dryden Press. All rights reserved.

holdings will exceed the targeted cash balance every month except for October and November, when shipments will be high but collections will not be coming in until later.

Based on the ratios in Table IC15-1, does it appear that SKI's target cash balance is appropriate? In addition to possibly lowering the target cash balance, what actions might SKI take to better improve its cash management policies, and how might that affect its EVA?

h. What reasons might SKI have for maintaining a relatively high amount of cash?

I. What are the three categories of inventory costs? If the company takes steps to reduce its inventory, what effect would this have on the various costs of holding inventory?

j. Is there any reason to think that SKI may be holding too much inventory? If so, how would that affect EVA and ROE?

k. If the company reduces its inventory without adversely affecting sales, what effect should this have on the company's cash position (1) in the short run and (2) in the long run? Explain in terms of the cash budget and the balance sheet.

l. Dan knows that SKI sells on the same credit terms as other firms in its industry. Use the ratios presented in Table IC15-1 to explain whether SKI's customers pay more or less promptly than those of its competitors. If there are differences, does that suggest that SKI should tighten or loosen its credit policy? What four variables make up a firm's credit policy, and in what direction should each be changed by SKI?

m. Does SKI face any risks if it tightens its credit policy?

n. If the company reduces its DSO without seriously affecting sales, what effect would this have on its cash position (1) in the short run and (2) in the long run? Answer in terms of the cash budget and the balance sheet. What effect would this have on EVA in the long run?

Copyright © 1996 by The Dryden Press. All rights reserved.

CHAPTER 15
Managing Current Assets

- Alternative Working Capital Policies
- Cash Management
- Inventory Management
- Accounts Receivable Management

Definitions:

- **Gross W.C.:** Total current assets.
- **Net W.C.:** Current assets - Current liabilities.
- **W.C. Policy:** Decisions as to (1) the level of each type of current asset, and (2) how current assets will be financed.
- **W.C. Mgt.:** Controlling cash, inventories, and A/R, plus S-T liability management.

Selected Ratios - SKI Inc.

	SKI	Industry
Current	1.75x	2.25x
Quick	0.83x	1.20x
Debt/Assets	58.76%	50.00%
Turnover of cash & securities	16.67x	22.22x
DSO (days)	45.00	32.00
Inv. turnover	4.82x	7.00x
F.A. turnover	11.35x	12.00x
T.A. turnover	2.08x	3.00x
Profit margin	2.07%	3.50%
ROE	10.45%	21.00%

SKI appears to have large amounts of working capital - given its level of sales.

BLUEPRINTS: CHAPTER 15

Copyright © 1996 by The Dryden Press. All rights reserved.

How does SKI's working capital policy compare with the industry?

- Working capital policy is reflected in current ratio, quick ratio, turnover of cash and securities, inventory turnover, and DSO.
- These ratios indicate SKI has large amounts of working capital relative to its level of sales. SKI is either very conservative or inefficient.

Is SKI inefficient or just conservative?

- A conservative policy may be appropriate if it leads to greater profitability.
- However, SKI is not as profitable as the average firm in the industry. This suggests the company has excessive working capital.

Cash doesn't earn a return, so why hold it?

1. Transactions: Must have some cash to operate.
2. Precaution: "Safety stock". But lessened by line of credit, marketable securities.
3. Compensating balances: For loans and/or services provided.
4. Speculation: To take advantage of bargains, to take discounts, etc. Reduced by credit lines, securities.

Copyright © 1996 by The Dryden Press. All rights reserved.

What's the goal of cash management?

- To meet above objectives, especially to have cash for transactions, yet not have any excess cash.

- Minimize transactions balances in particular, and also needs for cash to meet other objectives.

Ways to Minimize Cash Holdings:

Use a lockbox.

Insist on wire transfers from customers.

Synchronize inflows and outflows.

Use a remote disbursement account.

(Continued)...

...Continued

Increase forecast accuracy to reduce need for "safety stock" of cash.

Hold marketable securities (also reduces need for "safety stock").

Negotiate a line of credit (also reduces need for "safety stock").

Copyright © 1996 by The Dryden Press. All rights reserved.

What is "Float" and how is it affected by the firm's cash manager?

- Float is the difference between cash as shown on the firm's books and on its bank's books.
- If SKI collects checks in 2 days but those to whom SKI writes checks don't process them for 6 days, then SKI will have 4 days of net float .
- If a firm with 4 days of net float writes and receives $1 million of checks per day, it would be able to operate with $4 million less capital than if it had zero net float.

Cash Budget: The primary cash management tool

- Purpose: Forecasts cash inflows, outflows, and ending cash balances. Used to plan loans needed or funds available to invest.
- Timing: Daily, weekly, or monthly, depending on purpose of forecast. Monthly for annual planning, daily for actual cash management.

Data Required for Cash Budget

1. Sales forecast.
2. Information on collections delay.
3. Forecast of purchases & payment terms.
4. Forecast of cash expenses, taxes, etc.
5. Initial cash on hand.
6. Target cash balance.

Copyright © 1996 by The Dryden Press. All rights reserved.

SKI's Cash Budget for January and February

	Net cash inflow	
	January	February
Collections	$67,651.95	$62,755.40
Purchases	44,603.75	36,472.65
Wages	6,690.56	5,470.90
Rent	2,500.00	2,500.00
Total Payments	$53,794.31	$44,443.55
Net CF	$13,857.64	$18,311.85

(Continued)...

...Continued

Cash Budget

	January	February
Cash at start	$ 3,000.00	$16,857.64
Net CF (Slide 15-13)	13,857.64	18,311.85
Cumulative cash	$16,857.64	$35,169.49
Less: target cash	1,500.00	1,500.00
Surplus	$15,357.64	$33,669.49

Should depreciation be explicitly included in the cash budget?

- No. Depreciation is a noncash charge. Only cash payments and receipts appear on cash budget.
- However, depreciation does affect taxes, which appear in the cash budget.

Copyright © 1996 by The Dryden Press. All rights reserved.

What are some other potential cash inflows besides collections?

Proceeds from the sale of fixed assets.

Proceeds from stock and bond sales.

Interest earned.

Court settlements.

How can interest earned or paid be incorporated into the cash budget?

Interest earned: Add line in the collections section.

Interest paid: Add line in the payments section.

Found as interest rate x surplus/loan part of cash budget for preceding month.

How could bad debts be worked into the cash budget?

Collections would be reduced by the amount of the bad debt losses.

For example, if the firm had 3% bad debt losses, collections would total only 97% of sales.

Lower collections would lead to higher borrowing requirements.

BLUEPRINTS: CHAPTER 15

Copyright © 1996 by The Dryden Press. All rights reserved.

SKI's forecasted cash budget indicates that the company's cash holdings will exceed the targeted cash balance every month, except for October and November.

- Cash Budget indicates the company is holding too much cash.
- SKI could improve its EVA by either investing cash in more productive assets, or by returning cash to its shareholders.

What reasons might SKI have for maintaining a relatively high amount of cash?

- If sales turn out to be considerably less than expected, SKI could face a cash shortfall.
- A company may choose to hold large amounts of cash if it does not have much faith in its sales forecast, or if it is very conservative.

Categories of Inventory Costs

Carrying Costs: Storage and handling costs, insurance, property taxes, depreciation, and obsolescence.

Ordering Costs: Cost of placing orders, shipping and handling costs.

Costs of Running Short: Loss of sales, loss of customer goodwill, and the disruption of production schedules.

Reducing the average amount of inventory generally reduces carrying costs, increases ordering costs, and may increase the costs of running short.

Copyright © 1996 by The Dryden Press. All rights reserved.

Is SKI holding too much inventory?

- SKI's inventory turnover (4.82) is considerably lower than the industry average (7.00). The firm is carrying a lot of inventory per dollar of sales.
- By holding excessive inventory the firm is increasing its costs which reduces its ROE. Moreover, this additional working capital must be financed, so EVA is also lowered.

If SKI reduces its inventory without adversely affecting sales, what effect will this have on its cash position?

- Short-run: Cash will increase as inventory purchases decline.
- Long-run: Company is likely to take steps to reduce its cash holdings.

Do SKI's customers pay more or less promptly than those of its competitors?

- SKI's DSO (45 days) is well above the industry average (32 days).
- SKI's customers are paying less promptly.
- SKI should consider tightening its credit policy in order to reduce its DSO.

Copyright © 1996 by The Dryden Press. All rights reserved.

Elements of Credit Policy

1. **Cash Discounts:** Lowers price. Attracts new customers and reduces DSO.

2. **Credit Period:** How long to pay? Shorter period reduces DSO and average A/R, but it may discourage sales.

3. **Credit Standards:** Tighter standards tend to reduce sales, but reduce bad debt expense. Fewer bad debts reduces DSO.

4. **Collection Policy:** How tough? Tougher policy will reduce DSO but may damage customer relationships.

Does SKI face any risk if it tightens its credit policy?

Yes! A tighter credit policy may discourage sales. Some customers may choose to go elsewhere if they are pressured to pay their bills sooner.

If SKI succeeds in reducing DSO without adversely affecting sales, what effect would this have on its cash position?

- **Short-run:** If customers pay sooner this increases cash holdings.

- **Long-run:** Over time, the company would hopefully invest the cash in more productive assets, or pay it out to shareholders. Both of these actions would increase EVA.

Copyright © 1996 by The Dryden Press. All rights reserved.

EXAM-TYPE PROBLEMS

1. Ziltest Company's treasurer had $1 million of excess funds which were invested in marketable securities. At the time the investment was made, it was known that the funds would be needed in 6 months to fund an ongoing construction project. Six-month T-bills with a face value of $10,000 sold for $9,708.74 to yield a 6 percent nominal annual rate. As an alternative, the treasurer could purchase 7% coupon, semiannual payment, 10-year Treasury bonds at par. Seeking to earn a higher yield, he purchased the T-bonds. At the end of 6 months, when the funds were needed for construction, interest rates had risen to 9.5% on the T-bonds. The treasurer was forced to liquidate the T-bond holdings at a lower price. What was the absolute value of the dollar difference between the T-bond's purchase price and selling price?

2. Which of the following statement completions is most correct? If the yield curve is upward sloping, then a firm's marketable securities portfolio, assumed to be held for liquidity purposes, should be

   a. Weighted toward long-term securities because they pay higher rates.

   b. Weighted toward short-term securities because they pay higher rates.

   c. Weighted toward U.S. Treasury securities to avoid interest rate risk.

   d. Weighted toward short-term securities to avoid interest rate risk.

   e. Balanced between long- and short-term securities to minimize the effects of either an upward or a downward shift in interest rates.

3. Which of the following statements is most correct?

   a. If a firm's volume of credit sales declines then its DSO will also decline.

   b. If a firm changes its credit terms from 1/20, net 40 days, to 2/10, net 60 days, the impact on sales can't be determined because the increase in the discount is offset by the longer net terms which tends to reduce sales.

   c. The DSO of a firm with seasonal sales can vary because while the sales per day figure is usually based on the total annual sales, the accounts receivable balance will be high or low depending on the season.

   d. An aging schedule is used to determine what portion of customers pay cash and what portion buy on credit.

Copyright © 1996 by The Dryden Press. All rights reserved.

e. Aging schedules can be constructed from the summary data provided in the firm's financial statements.

4. Jarrett Enterprises is considering whether to pursue a restricted or relaxed current asset investment policy. The firm's annual sales are $400,000; its fixed assets are $100,000; debt and equity are each 50% of total assets. EBIT is $36,000, the interest rate on the firm's debt is 10%, and the firm's tax rate is 40%. With a restricted policy, current assets will be 15% of sales. Under a relaxed policy, current assets will be 25% of sales. What is the difference in the projected ROEs between the restricted and relaxed policies?

5. Porta Stadium Inc. has annual sales of $40,000,000 and keeps average inventory of $10,000,000. On average the firm has accounts receivable of $8,000,000. The firm buys all raw materials on credit and its trade credit terms are net 30 days. It pays on time. The firm's managers are searching for ways to shorten the cash conversion cycle. If sales can be maintained at existing levels but inventory can be lowered by $2,000,000 and accounts receivable lowered by $1,000,000, what will be the net change in the cash conversion cycle? Use a 360-day year. (Hint: See Appendix 15A.)

Copyright © 1996 by The Dryden Press. All rights reserved.

16-13 Bats and Balls (B&B) Inc., a baseball equipment manufacturer, is a small company with seasonal sales. Each year before the baseball season, B&B purchases inventory which is financed through a combination of trade credit and short-term bank loans. At the end of the season, B&B uses sales revenues to repay its short-term obligations. The company is always looking for ways to become more profitable, and senior management has asked one of its employees, Ann Taylor, to review the company's current asset financing policies. Putting together her report, Ann is trying to answer each of the following questions.

a. B&B tries to match the maturity of its assets and liabilities. Describe how B&B could adopt a more aggressive or more conservative financing policy.

b. What are the advantages and disadvantages of using short-term credit as a source of financing?

c. Is it likely that B&B could make significantly greater use of accruals?

d. Assume that B&B buys on terms of 1/10, net 30, but that it can get away with paying on the 40th day if it chooses not to take discounts. Also, assume that it purchases $3 million of components per year, net of discounts. How much free trade credit can the company get, how much costly trade credit can it get, and what is the percentage cost of the costly credit? Should B&B take discounts?

e. Would it be feasible for B&B to finance with commercial paper?

f. Suppose B&B decided to raise an additional $100,000 as a 1-year loan from its bank, for which it was quoted a rate of 8 percent. What is the effective annual cost rate assuming (1) simple interest, (2) discount interest, (3) discount interest with a 10 percent compensating balance, and (4) add-on interest on a 12-month installment loan? For the first 3 of these assumptions, would it matter if the loan were for 90 days, but renewable, rather than for a year?

g. How large would the loan actually be in each of the cases in Part f?

h. What are the pros and cons of borrowing on a secured versus an unsecured basis? If inventories or receivables are to be used as collateral, how would the loan be handled?

Copyright © 1996 by The Dryden Press. All rights reserved.

Chapter 16
Financing Current Assets

- Working Capital Financing Policies
- A/P (Trade Credit)
- Commercial Paper
- S-T Bank Loans

Working Capital Financing Policies:

- **Moderate:** Match the maturity of the assets with the maturity of the financing.

- **Aggressive:** Use short-term financing to finance permanent assets.

- **Conservative:** Use permanent capital for permanent assets and temporary assets.

Moderate Financing Policy

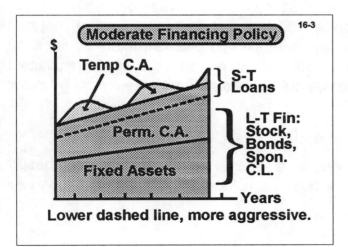

Lower dashed line, more aggressive.

Copyright © 1996 by The Dryden Press. All rights reserved.

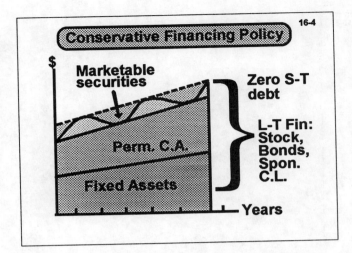

Conservative Financing Policy 16-4

$

Marketable securities

Perm. C.A.

Fixed Assets

Zero S-T debt

L-T Fin: Stock, Bonds, Spon. C.L.

Years

16-5

What is short-term credit, and what are the major sources?

- **S-T credit:** Any debt scheduled for repayment within one year.
- **Major sources:**
  - Accounts payable (trade credit)
  - Bank loans
  - Commercial paper
  - Accruals

16-6

- **Is S-T credit riskier than L-T?**
  To company, yes. Required repayment always looms. May have trouble rolling over loans.

- **Advantages of short-term credit:**
  Low cost--visualize yield curve.
  Can get funds relatively quickly.
  Can repay without penalty.

Copyright © 1996 by The Dryden Press. All rights reserved.

Is there a cost to accruals? Do firms have much control over amount of accruals?

- Accruals are free in that no explicit interest is charged.
- Firms have little control over the level of accruals. Levels are influenced more by industry custom, economic forces, and tax laws.

What is trade credit?

- Trade credit is credit furnished by a firm's suppliers.
- Trade credit is often the largest source of short-term credit, especially for small firms.
- Spontaneous, easy to get, but cost can be high.

B&B buys $3,030,303 gross, or $3,000,000 net, on terms of 1/10, net 30, and pays on Day 40. How much free and costly trade credit, and what's the cost of costly trade credit?

Net daily purchases = $3,000,000/360
= $8,333.

Copyright © 1996 by The Dryden Press. All rights reserved.

Gross/Net Breakdown

- Company buys goods worth $3,000,000. That's the cash price.
- They must pay $30,303 more if they don't take discounts.
- Think of the extra $30,303 as a financing cost similar to interest on a loan.
- Want to compare that cost with the cost of a bank loan.

Payables level if take discount:
Payables = $8,333(10) = $83,333.

Payables level if don't take discount:
Payables = $8,333(40) = $333,333.

Credit Breakdown:
Total trade credit	= $333,333
Free trade credit	= 83,333
Costly trade credit	= $250,000

Nominal cost of costly trade credit:

Firm loses 0.01($3,030,303) = $30,303 of discounts to obtain $250,000 in extra trade credit, so

$$k_{Nom} = \frac{\$30,303}{\$250,000} = 0.1212 = 12.12\%.$$

But the $30,303 is paid all <u>during</u> the year, not at year-end, so EAR rate is higher.

BLUEPRINTS: CHAPTER 16

Copyright © 1996 by The Dryden Press. All rights reserved.

Nominal cost formula, 1/10, net 40:

$$k_{Nom} = \frac{Dis.}{1 - Dis.} \times \frac{360}{Days\ taken - Dis.\ per.}$$

$$= \frac{1}{99} \times \frac{360}{30} = 0.0101 \times 12$$

$$= 0.1212 = 12.12\%.$$

Pays 1.01% 12 times per year.

Effective annual rate, 1/10, net 40:

Periodic rate = 0.01/0.99 = 1.01%.

Periods/year = 360/(40 - 10) = 12.

$$EAR = (1 + Periodic\ rate)^n - 1.0$$
$$= (1.0101)^{12} - 1.0 = 12.82\%$$

Commercial Paper (CP)

- Short-term notes issued by large, strong companies. B&B couldn't issue CP--it's too small.

- CP trades in the market at rates just above T-bill rate.

- CP is bought with surplus cash by banks and other companies, then held as a marketable security for liquidity purposes.

Copyright © 1996 by The Dryden Press. All rights reserved.

A bank is willing to lend B&B $100,000 for 1 year at an 8 percent nominal rate. What is the EAR under the following five loans?

1. Simple annual interest, 1 year.

2. Simple interest, paid monthly.

3. Discount interest.

4. Discount interest with 10 percent compensating balance.

5. Installment loan, add-on, 12 months.

Why must we use EAR to evaluate the alternative loans?

- Nominal (quoted) rate = 8% in all cases.

- We want to compare loan cost rates and choose lowest cost loan.

- We must make comparison on EAR = Equivalent (or Effective) Annual Rate basis.

Simple annual interest, 1-year loan:

"Simple interest" means not discount or add-on.

Interest = 0.08($100,000) = $8,000.

$$k_{Nom} = EAR = \frac{\$8,000}{\$100,000} = 0.08 = 8.0\%$$

On a simple interest loan of one year, k_{Nom} = EAR.

Copyright © 1996 by The Dryden Press. All rights reserved.

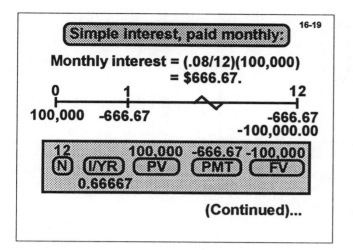

Simple interest, paid monthly: 16-19

Monthly interest = (.08/12)(100,000)
= \$666.67.

```
0            1                         12
├───────────┼────────────/\/──────────┤
100,000   -666.67                  -666.67
                                -100,000.00
```

```
  12         100,000   -666.67  -100,000
 (N)  (I/YR)   (PV)    (PMT)     (FV)
     0.66667
```

(Continued)...

16-20

$$k_{Nom} = \text{(monthly rate)(12)}$$
$$= 0.66667(12) = \boxed{8.00\%}$$

$$EAR = \left(1 + \frac{0.08}{12}\right)^{12} - 1 = \boxed{8.30\%}$$

or: 8 ■ NOM%, 12 ■ P/YR, ■ EFF% = 8.30%

Note: If interest were paid quarterly, then

$$EAR = \left(1 + \frac{0.08}{4}\right)^{4} - 1 = 8.24\%$$

Daily, EAR = 8.33%.

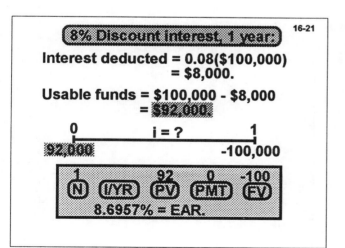

8% Discount interest, 1 year: 16-21

Interest deducted = 0.08(\$100,000)
= \$8,000.

Usable funds = \$100,000 - \$8,000
= \$92,000

```
0           i = ?              1
├──────────────────────────────┤
92,000                      -100,000
```

```
  1              92      0     -100
 (N)  (I/YR)   (PV)   (PMT)    (FV)
     8.6957% = EAR.
```

BLUEPRINTS: CHAPTER 16

Copyright © 1996 by The Dryden Press. All rights reserved.

Discount interest (cont.):

$$\text{Formula rate* (discount)} = \frac{\text{Nominal rate (decimal)}}{1 - \text{Nominal rate (decimal)}}$$

$$= \frac{0.08}{1 - 0.08} = 8.6957\%.$$

$$\text{Amt. borrowed} = \frac{\text{Amount needed}}{1 - \text{Nominal rate (decimal)}}$$

$$= \frac{\$100,000}{0.92} = \$108,696.$$

*Correct only for 1-year loan.

Need $100,000. Offered loan with terms of 8% discount interest, 10% compensating balance:

$$\text{Face amt of loan} = \frac{\text{Amount needed}}{1 - \text{Nom rate} - \text{CB}}$$

$$= \frac{\$100,000}{1 - 0.08 - 0.1} = \$121,951.$$

(Continued)...

Interest = 0.08($121,951) = $9,756.

$$\text{Cost} = \frac{\text{Interest paid}}{\text{Amount received}}$$

$$\text{EAR} = \frac{\$9,756}{\$100,000} = 9.756\%$$

EAR correct only if borrow for 1 year.

(Continued)...

BLUEPRINTS: CHAPTER 16

Copyright © 1996 by The Dryden Press. All rights reserved.

8% discount interest with 10% compensating balance (cont.):

$$\text{Formula rate} = \frac{\text{Nominal rate (decimal)}}{1 - \text{Nom. rate} - \text{CB}}$$

$$= \frac{0.08}{1 - 0.08 - 0.10}$$

$$= 9.756\%.$$

EAR only if borrow for 1 year.

(Continued)...

Time Line Set-up:

```
0              i=?              1
|------------------------------|
```

121,951 Loan	-121,951
- 9,756 Prepaid interest	+ 12,195
- 12,195 CB	-109,756
100,000 Usable funds	

```
  1        100,000      0    -109,756
 (N)  (I/YR)   (PV)   (PMT)   (FV)
         9.756% = EAR
```

This procedure can handle variations.

1- year installment loan, 8% "add-on":

Interest = 0.08($100,000) = $8,000.

Face amount = $100,000 + $8,000 = $108,000.

Monthly payment = $108,000/12 = $9,000.

Average loan outstanding = $100,000/2 = $50,000.

Approximate cost = $8,000/$50,000 = 16.0%.

Copyright © 1996 by The Dryden Press. All rights reserved.

Installment loan (cont.):

To find the EAR, recognize that the firm has received $100,000 and must make monthly payments of $9,000. This constitutes an ordinary annuity as shown below:

months

0	i = ?	1	2		12
100,000		-9,000	-9,000		-9,000

12		100,000	-9,000	0
(N)	(I/YR)	(PV)	(PMT)	(FV)

1.2043% = rate per month

k_{Nom} = APR = (1.2043)(12) = **14.45%**

EAR = (1.012043)^{12} - 1 = **15.45%**

14.45 ■ NOM ⟶ enters nom rate

12 ■ P/YR ⟶ enters 12 pmts/yr

■ EFF% = 15.4489 = **15.45%**

1 ■ P/YR to reset calculator

What is a secured loan?

- In a secured loan, the borrower pledges assets as collateral for the loan.
- For short-term loans, the most commonly pledged assets are receivables and inventories.

Securities are great collateral, but generally not available.

BLUEPRINTS: CHAPTER 16

Copyright © 1996 by The Dryden Press. All rights reserved.

What are the differences between pledging and factoring receivables?

- If receivables are pledged, the lender has recourse against both the original buyer of the goods and the borrower.

- When receivables are factored, they are generally sold, and the buyer (lender) has no recourse to the borrower.

What are the three forms of inventory financing?

- Blanket lien.
- Trust receipt.
- Warehouse receipt.
- The form used depends on the type of inventory and situation at hand.

Legal stuff is vital:

- Security agreement: Standard form under Uniform Commercial Code. Describes when lender can claim collateral.

- UCC Form-1: Filed with Secretary of State to establish claim. Future lenders do search, won't lend if prior UCC-1 is on file.

Copyright © 1996 by The Dryden Press. All rights reserved.

EXAM-TYPE PROBLEMS

1. The Lasser Company needs to finance an increase in its working capital for the coming year. Lasser is reviewing the following three options: (1) The firm can borrow from its bank on a simple interest basis for one year at 13%. (2) It can borrow on a 3-month, but renewable, loan at a 12% nominal rate. The loan is a simple interest loan, completely paid off at the end of each quarter, then renewed for another quarter. (3) The firm can increase its accounts payable by not taking discounts. Lasser buys on credit terms of 1/30, net 60 days. What is the effective annual cost (not the approximate cost) of the least expensive type of credit, assuming 360 days per year?

2. Which of the following statements is most correct?

   a. Under normal conditions the shape of the yield curve implies that the interest cost of short-term debt is greater than that of long-term debt, although short-term debt has other advantages that make it desirable as a financing source.

   b. Flexibility is an advantage of short-term credit but this is somewhat offset by the higher flotation costs associated with the need to repeatedly renew short-term credit.

   c. A short-term loan can usually be obtained more quickly than a long-term loan but the penalty for early repayment of a short-term loan is significantly higher than for a long-term loan.

   d. Statements about the flexibility, cost, and riskiness of short-term versus long-term credit are dependent on the type of credit that is actually used.

   e. Short-term debt is often less costly than long-term debt and the major reason for this is that short-term debt exposes the borrowing firm to much less risk than long-term debt.

Copyright © 1996 by The Dryden Press. All rights reserved.

SOLUTIONS TO EXAM-TYPE PROBLEMS

CHAPTER 1

1. d.

2. e.

CHAPTER 2

1. b.

2. *Florida muni bond*

   A-T yield on FLA bond = 8%. (The munis are tax exempt.)

   AT&T bond

   A-T yield on AT&T bond = 11% - Taxes = 11% - 11%(0.4) = 6.6%.

   Alternate solution

   Invest $20,000 @ 11% = $2,200 interest.
   Pay 40% tax, so A-T income = $2,200(1 - T) = $2,200(0.6) = $1,320.
   A-T rate of return = $1,320/$20,000 = 6.6%.

   AT&T preferred stock

   A-T yield = 9% - Taxes = 9% - 0.3(9%)(0.4) = 9% - 1.08% = 7.92%.

   Therefore, invest in the Florida muni bonds which yield 8% after taxes. Note: This problem can be made harder by asking for the tax rate that would cause the company to prefer the AT&T bonds or the preferred stock.

CHAPTER 3

1. ROE = Profit margin × Total assets turnover × Equity multiplier
      = NI/Sales × Sales/TA × TA/Equity.

   Now we need to determine the inputs for the equation from the data that were given. On the left we set up an income statement, and we put numbers in it on the right:

Sales (given)	$20,000
– Cost	NA
EBIT (given)	$ 2,000
– Interest (given)	500
EBT	$ 1,500
– Taxes (30%)	450
Net income	$ 1,050

Copyright © 1996 by The Dryden Press. All rights reserved.

Now we can use some ratios to get some more data:

Total assets turnover = S/TA = 2.5 (given).

D/A = 70%, so E/A = 30%, and therefore TA/E = 1/(E/A) = 1/0.3 = 3.33.

Now we can complete the Du Pont equation to determine ROE:

ROE = \$1,050/\$20,000 × 2.5 × 3.33 = 43.75%.

2.(a) Current NI = NI = 0.05 × \$5,000,000 = \$250,000.

Current ROE = NI/Equity = \$250,000/\$4,000,000 = 6.25%.

Current DSO = Receivables/(Sales/360) = \$2,250,000/(\$5,000,000/360) = 162 days.

Reduce DSO to 60 days. Frees up cash:

102 × \$5,000,000/360 = \$1,416,667.

Alternatively,

Accounts receivable/(\$5,000,000/360) = 60
                    Accounts receivable = \$833,333.

Δ in A/R = \$2,250,000 - \$833,333 = \$1,416,667.

Reduce Common Equity:

\$4,000,000 - \$1,416,667 = \$2,583,333.

New ROE = \$250,000/\$2,583,333 = 9.68%.

Change in ROE = 9.68% - 6.25% = 3.43%.

(b) [1] Doubling the dollar amounts would not affect the answer; it would still be 3.43%.

[2] Target DSO = 70 days.
Freed up cash = 92 × \$5,000,000/360 = \$1,277,778.

Reduce Common Equity: \$4,000,000 - \$1,277,778 = \$2,722,222.
New ROE = \$250,000/\$2,722,222 = 9.18%.

Change in ROE = 9.18% - 6.25% = 2.93%.

[3] This would provide the same answer as in Part a.
Sales/Receivables = 6
\$5,000,000/Receivables = 6
Receivables = \$5,000,000/6 = \$833,333.

Thus, receivables would be reduced by \$1,416,667.

Copyright © 1996 by The Dryden Press. All rights reserved.

[4]   Original EPS = NI/Shares = $250,000/250,000 = $1.00.

New EPS calculation: Assume book value = Market value. (M/B = 1).
Price = $4,000,000/250,000 shares = $16. Stock is selling for $16
per share.

Thus, must buy back $1,416,667/$16 = 88,542 shares.

Number of shares outstanding = 250,000 - 88,542 = 161,458.

New EPS = $250,000/161,458 = $1.55.

Δ in EPS = $1.55 - $1.00 = $0.55 per share.

[5]   From Part 4, book value = $16 per share.
Market value = 2 × $16 = $32.

Thus, firm must buy back $1,416,667/$32 = 44,271 shares.
Number of shares outstanding = 250,000 - 44,271 = 205,729 shares.

New EPS = $250,000/205,729 = $1.22.

Δ in EPS = $1.22 - $1.00 = $0.22 per share.

(c) We could have started with lower receivables and higher fixed assets or
inventory, then had you calculate the fixed assets or inventory turnover
ratios, then move to lower fixed assets or inventory turnover reducing
equity by like amounts, and then determining the effects on ROE and EPS
under different conditions. In any of these cases, we could have used the
funds generated to retire debt, which would have lowered interest charges
and consequently increased net income and EPS. (Note that information
would have had to been given on interest and EBIT too.)
        If we had to increase assets, then we would have had to finance this
increase by adding either debt or equity, which would have lowered ROE and
EPS, other things held constant.

3.   a.

4.   TIE = EBIT/I, so find EBIT and I.
Interest = $800,000 × 0.1 = $80,000.
Net income = $3,200,000 × 0.06 = $192,000.
Pre-tax income = $192,000/(1 - T) = $192,000/0.6 = $320,000.
EBIT = $320,000 + $80,000 = $400,000.
TIE = $400,000/$80,000 = 5.0×.

5.   Before: Equity multiplier = 1/(1 - D/A) = 1/(1 - 0.5) = 2.0.
ROE = (PM)(Assets turnover)(EM) = (10%)(0.25)(2.0) = 5%,
After: [ROE = 2(5%) = 10%]:
        10% = (12%)(0.25)(EM)
        EM = 3.33 = TA/TE = 3.33/1.00.
        TA = TD + TE
        3.33 = TD + 1.00
        TD = 2.33.
Debt ratio = 2.33/3.33 = 0.70 = 70%.

Copyright © 1996 by The Dryden Press. All rights reserved.

CHAPTER 4

1.   e.

2.   First, note that we will use the equation $k_t = 4\% + IP_t + MRP_t$. We have the
      data needed to find the IPs:

      $IP_5 = (9\% + 6\% + 4\% + 4\% + 4\%)/5 = 27\%/5 = 5.4\%$.
      $IP_2 = (9\% + 6\%)/2 = 7.5\%$.

      Now we can substitute into the equation:

      $k_5 = 4\% + 5.4\% + MRP = 12\%$.
      $k_2 = 4\% + 7.5\% + MRP = 12\%$.

      Now we can solve for the MRPs, and find the difference between them:

      $MRP_5 = 12\% - 9.4\% = 2.6\%$.
      $MRP_2 = 12\% - 11.5\% = 0.5\%$.   Difference = (2.6% - 0.5%) = 2.1%.

CHAPTER 5

1.   a.

2.   c.

3.   Before: $1.15 = 0.95(b_R) + 0.05(1.0)$
             $0.95(b_R) = 1.10$
                  $b_R = 1.158$.

      After: $b_P = 0.95(b_R) + 0.05(2.0) = 1.10 + 0.10 = 1.20$.

CHAPTER 6

1.   d.

2.   Time line:

      Tabular solution:

      Price of car on 27th birthday

      $FV = \$25,000(FVIF_{10\%,7}) = \$25,000(1.9487) = \$48,718$.

Copyright © 1996 by The Dryden Press. All rights reserved.

Annual investment required

$$FV \text{ of annuity} = FVA_n = PMT(FVIFA_{i,n})$$
$$\$48,718 = PMT(FVIFA_{14\%,7})$$
$$PMT = \$48,718/10.7305 = \$4,540.14.$$

Financial calculator solution:

Price of car on 27th birthday

Inputs: N = 7; I = 10; PV = –25,000; PMT = 0.
Output: FV = $48,717.93 ≈ $48,718.

Annual investment required

Inputs: N = 7; I = 14; PV = 0; FV = 48,718.
Output: PMT = –$4,540.15.

3. **Time line:**

```
        1/1/95                                          1/1/00
         0      10%   1        2        3        4       5    Years
         |–––––––––|––––––––|––––––––|––––––––|––––––––|
PMT = 8,000    8,000    8,000    8,000    8,000    FV_Plan = ?
                                  –5,000   –5,000   –5,000
                                                    FV_Withdrawals = ?
```

Tabular solution:

Easy way $5,000(FVIFA_{10\%,3}) = \$5,000(3.3100) = \$16,550.$

Hard way Target FV = $8,000(FVIFA_{10\%,5})(1.10) = \$53,725.$ Find FV of cash flow stream of $8,000 for Years 0-2; $3,000, for Years 3-4; and –$5,000 for Year 5; and subtract from $53,725. The answer is $16,550.

Financial calculator solution:

Calculate the FV of the withdrawals which is how much her actual account fell short of her plan.

END mode   Inputs: N = 3; I = 10; PV = 0; PMT = –5,000.
           Output: FV = $16,550.

Alternative solution: *Calculate FV of original plan.*

BEGIN mode   Inputs: N = 5; I = 10; PV = 0; PMT = –8,000.
             Output: FV = $53,724.88.

Calculate FV of actual deposits less withdrawals, take the difference.

Inputs: $CF_0 = 8,000$; $CF_1 = 8,000$; $N_j = 2$; $CF_2 = 3,000$; $N_j = 2$;
          $CF_3 = -5,000$; I = 10.
Output: NFV = $37,174.88.
Difference: $53,724.88 – $37,174.88 = $16,550.

Copyright © 1996 by The Dryden Press. All rights reserved.

4.   **Time line:**

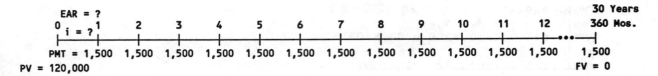

EAR = ?

0 i = ? 1   2   3   4   5   6   7   8   9   10   11   12   ...   30 Years
                                                                  360 Mos.

PMT = 1,500 1,500 1,500 1,500 1,500 1,500 1,500 1,500 1,500 1,500 1,500 1,500 1,500

PV = 120,000   FV = 0

Financial calculator solution:

Calculate periodic rate

Inputs: N = 360; PV = −120,000; PMT = 1,500; FV = 0.
Output: I = 1.235% per period.

Use interest rate conversion feature

Inputs: NOM% = 1.235 × 12 = 14.82; P/YR = 12.
Output: EFF% = 15.868% ≈ 15.87%.

5.   **Steps:**

(1)   He will save for 10 years, then receive payments for 25 years.

(2)   He wants payments of $40,000 per year in today's dollars for first payment only. Real income will decline. Inflation will be 5%. Enter N = 10, I = 5, PV = −40,000, PMT = 0, and press FV to get FV = $65,155.79.

(3)   He now has $100,000 in an account which pays 8%, annual compounding. We need to find the FV of the $100,000 after 10 years. Enter N = 10, I = 8, PV = −100,000, PMT = 0, and press FV to get FV = $215,892.50.

(4)   He wants to withdraw, or have payments of, $65,155.79 per year for 25 years, with the first payment made at the beginning of the first retirement year. So, we have a 25-year annuity due with PMT = $65,155.79, at an interest rate of 8%. (The interest rate is 8% annually, so no adjustment is required.) Set the calculator to BEGIN MODE, then enter N = 25, I = 8, PMT = 65,155.79, FV = 0, and press PV to get PV = $751,165.35. This amount must be on hand to make the 25 payments.

(5)   Since the original $100,000, which grows to $215,892.50, will be available, we must save enough to accumulate $751,165.35. Need $751,165.35 − $215,892.50 = $535,272.85.

(6)   The $535,272.85 is the FV of a 10-year ordinary annuity. The payments will be deposited in the bank and earn 8% interest. Therefore, set the calculator to END MODE and enter N = 10, I = 8, PV = 0, FV = 535,272.85, and press PMT to find PMT = $36,949.61 = $36,950.

Copyright © 1996 by The Dryden Press. All rights reserved.

CHAPTER 7

1.   **Time line:**

Investors would expect to earn either the YTM or the YTC, and the expected
return on the old bonds is the cost GSU would have to pay in order to sell
new bonds.

Financial calculator solution:

Calculate the YTM on the old bonds:

Inputs: N = 2(30) = 60; PV = -676.77; PMT = 80/2 = 40; FV = 1,000.
Output: I = 6% = $k_d/2$.   6% is the semiannual or periodic rate.
YTM = 2(6%) = 12%.

Calculate the YTC for comparison:

Inputs: N = 2(5) = 10; PV = -676.77; PMT = 80/2 = 40; FV = 1,080.
Output: I = 9.70% = $k_d/2$.
YTC = 2(9.70%) = 19.40%.

Would investors expect the company to call the bonds?   No.   The company
currently pays 8% on its debt.   New debt would cost GSU at least 12%.   It
would be foolish for the company to call the bonds, thus investors would
logically expect to earn the current YTM of 12% on new bonds.   So k_d = 12%
is the best estimate of the nominal annual interest rate GSU would have to
pay on the new bonds.

2.   **Time line:**

Financial calculator solution:

We are comparing securities with different payment patterns, semiannual
and quarterly.   To properly value the student loan securities, we must
match the opportunity cost rate on the bonds with the payment period on
the student loan securities, which is semiannual.   Thus, convert the
quarterly (periodic) rate to a semiannual effective rate.
     Since the bonds are selling at par value, the 9% coupon rate is also
the market rate.   The semiannual periodic rate is then 9%/2 = 4.5%.   There
are 2 compounding periods (quarters) in a half year.

Copyright © 1996 by The Dryden Press. All rights reserved.

*Calculate the opportunity cost semiannual EAR of the quarterly payment
bonds (using interest rate conversion feature):*

Inputs: P/YR = 2; NOM% = 9/2 = 4.5.
Output: EFF% = 4.55% = semiannual effective rate.

*Calculate the present value of the student loan package, V_B, using the
semiannual effective rate (using cash flows):*

Inputs: CF_0 = 0; CF_1 = 40; N_j = 10; CF_2 = 50; N_j = 13; CF_3 = 1,050;
          I = 4.55.
Output: NPV = $985.97 = V_B.

3. **Time line:**

Calculate the nominal yield to call: The bonds are selling at a premium
because the coupon interest rate is above the market rate. Under the
expectation of a flat yield curve, the bonds will most likely be called so
that the firm can issue new, cheaper bonds. The FV is the call price and
the period is 5 years or 10 semiannual periods.

Financial calculator solution:

Calculate the semiannual interest rate and convert to nominal annual rate.

Inputs: N = 10; PV = -1,230.51; PMT = 60; FV = 1,080.
Output: I = 3.85 periodic rate (semiannual).

The nominal annual rate equals 2 × 3.85% = 7.70%. Thus, the before-tax
cost of debt is 7.70%.

4. **Time line:**

Financial calculator solution:

Calculate the original YTM when the bonds were issued.

Inputs: N = 20; PV = -214.50; PMT = 0; FV = 1,000. Output: I = 8.0%.

Copyright © 1996 by The Dryden Press. All rights reserved.

Calculate the current market rate using the current market price of $239.39.

Inputs: N = 15; PV = -239.39; PMT = 0; FV = 1,000. Output: I = 10.0%.

At a current market price of $239.39, market rates are 10.0%. Since market rates have risen, the bond will not likely be called. So today, at Year 5, the YTM of 10% is the most likely annual rate of return an investor who buys the bonds today will earn.

5. e.

6. d.

CHAPTER 8

1. <u>Step 1</u> *Calculate required rate of return*

$$k_s = \frac{\$2}{\$20} + 6\% = 10\% + 6\% = 16\%.$$

<u>Step 2</u> *Calculate risk-free rate*

$$16\% = k_{RF} + (15\% - k_{RF})1.2$$
$$k_{RF} = 10\%.$$

<u>Step 3</u> *Calculate capital gain*

New $k_s = 10\% + (15\% - 10\%)0.6 = 13\%.$

$$\hat{P}_{New} = \frac{\$2}{0.13 - 0.06} = \$28.57.$$

Therefore, the percentage capital gain is 43%:

$$\frac{\$28.57 - \$20.00}{\$20.00} = \frac{\$8.57}{\$20.00} = 43\%.$$

2. **Time line:**

BLUEPRINTS: SOLUTIONS

Copyright © 1996 by The Dryden Press. All rights reserved.

Tabular solution:

$\hat{P}_0$ = \$0.48(PVIF$_{10\%,1}$) + \$0.576(PVIF$_{10\%,2}$) + \$0.691(PVIF$_{10\%,3}$) + \$93.32(PVIF$_{10\%,3}$)
= \$0.48(0.9091) + \$0.576(0.8264) + \$0.691(0.7513) + \$93.32(0.7513)
= \$0.436 + \$0.476 + \$0.519 + \$70.113 = \$71.54.

Financial calculator solution:

Inputs: CF_0 = 0; CF_1 = 0.48; CF_2 = 0.576; CF_3 = 94.011; I = 10.
Output: NPV = \$71.54. $\hat{P}_0$ = \$71.54.

3.   e.

CHAPTER 9

1.   **Time line:**

V_B = 686.86   FV = 1,000

Financial calculator solution:

Calculate the <u>nominal</u> YTM of the bond:

Inputs: N = 80; PV = −686.86; PMT = 20; FV = 1,000.
Output: I = 3.05% periodic rate = quarterly rate.

Nominal annual rate = 3.05% × 4 = 12.20%.

Calculate k_d *after-tax:* $k_{d,AT}$ = 12.20%(1 − T) = 12.20%(1 − 0.4) = 7.32%.

2.   Information given:

Net income = \$600; Debt = 0.4; Equity = 0.6; Dividend payout = 0.6.

Calculate the retained earnings break point:

Breakpoint$_{RE}$ = Retained earnings/Equity fraction
= \$600(1 − 0.6)/0.6 = \$240/0.6 = \$400.

Since the \$600 capital budget exceeds the retained earnings breakpoint, BP$_{RE}$ = \$400, Allison will need new equity capital. The firm will have \$240 of retained earnings which will be exhausted when the capital budget reaches \$400.

Copyright © 1996 by The Dryden Press. All rights reserved.

Use the dividend growth model to calculate k_e:

$$k_e = \frac{D_0(1 + g)}{P_0(1 - F)} + g = \frac{\$2.20(1.06)}{\$28(1 - 0.15)} + 0.06 = \frac{\$2.33}{\$23.80} + 0.06$$

$$= 0.0980 + 0.06 = 0.1580 = 15.8\%.$$

3. <u>Step 1.</u> Calculate the break point for retained earnings, BP_{RE}:

$$BP_{RE} = \frac{\text{Retained earnings}}{\text{Equity fraction}} = \frac{NI(1 - \text{Payout})}{0.45} = \frac{\$50(0.6)}{0.45} = \$66.67 \text{ million.}$$

Note that we are interested in the WACC at a capital budget of \$100 million. The MCC or $WACC_2$ at this point will require use of new equity, k_e.

<u>Step 2.</u> Calculate cost of new equity, k_e:

$$k_e = \frac{D_1}{P_0(1 - F)} + g = \frac{\$3.00(1.10)}{\$50(1 - 0.15)} + 0.10$$

$$= \frac{\$3.30}{\$42.50} + 0.10 = 0.0776 + 0.10 = 0.1776 = 17.76\%.$$

<u>Step 3.</u> Use target capital structure weights to calculate $WACC_2$.

$$WACC_2 = 0.55(6.5\%) + 0.45(17.76\%) = 11.57\%.$$

Note that the initial $WACC_1$ is 11.05% and is calculated as follows:

Debt: $k_{d,AT} = 10.0\%(1 - 0.35) = 6.50\%.$

Retained earnings: $k_s = D_1/P_0 + g = \$3.00(1.10)/\$50.00 + 0.10$
$$= 0.066 + 0.10 = 0.1660 = 16.60\%.$$

Copyright © 1996 by The Dryden Press. All rights reserved.

$$WACC_1 = 0.55(6.50\%) + 0.45(16.60\%) = 3.575\% + 7.47\% = 11.045\% \approx 11.05\%.$$

CHAPTER 10

1. **Time line:**

$$NPV_S = ? \quad IRR_S = ?$$

$$NPV_L = ? \quad IRR_L = ?$$

Financial calculator solution:

Calculate the NPV and IRR of each project then select the IRR of the higher NPV project.

Project S; Inputs: $CF_0 = -1,100$; $CF_1 = 900$; $CF_2 = 350$; $CF_3 = 50$; $CF_4 = 10$; I = 12
Output: $NPV_S = \$24.53$; $IRR_S = 13.88\%$.

Project L; Inputs: $CF_0 = -1,100$; $CF_1 = 0$; $CF_2 = 300$; $CF_3 = 500$; $CF_4 = 850$; I = 12
Output: $NPV_L = \$35.24$; $IRR_L = 13.09\%$.

Project L has the higher NPV and its IRR = 13.09%.

2. **Time line:**

$$IRR_A = ?$$
$$IRR_B = ?$$

	0	1	2	3	4 Years
CF_X	-100	50	40	30	10
CF_Y	-100	10	30	40	60
CF_{X-Y}	0	40	10	-10	-50

Financial calculator solution:

Calculate the IRR of each project.

Project X

Inputs: $CF_0 = -100$; $CF_1 = 50$; $CF_2 = 40$; $CF_3 = 30$; $CF_4 = 10$.
Output: IRR = 14.489% ≈ 14.49%.

Project Y

Inputs: $CF_0 = -100$; $CF_1 = 10$; $CF_2 = 30$; $CF_3 = 40$; $CF_4 = 60$.
Output: IRR = 11.79%.

Copyright © 1996 by The Dryden Press. All rights reserved.

Calculate the NPVs of the projects at k = 0 discount rate.

$NPV_{X,k=0\%}$ = -\$100 + \$50 + \$40 + \$30 + \$10 = \$30.

$NPV_{Y,k=0\%}$ = -\$100 + \$10 + \$30 + \$40 + \$60 = \$40.

Calculate the IRR of the residual project cash flows, i.e., Project$_{X-Y}$

IRR_{X-Y} Inputs: CF_0 = 0; CF_1 = 40; CF_2 = 10; CF_3 = -10; CF_4 = -50.
                 Output: IRR = 7.167% ≈ 7.17%.

Using the calculator we can determine that there is a crossover point in the relevant part of the NPV profile graph. Project X has the higher IRR. Project Y has the higher NPV at k = 0. The crossover rate is 7.17% and occurs in the upper right quadrant.

3.   **Time line:**

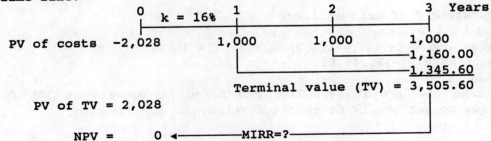

Copyright © 1996 by The Dryden Press. All rights reserved.

Step 1: *Calculate the historical beta.*

Regression method: **Financial calculator:** Different calculators have different list entry procedures and key stroke sequences. (Refer to your calculator manual.)

Enter Nulook returns as the y-list:

Inputs: Item(1) = 9 INPUT; Item(2) = 15 INPUT; Item(3) = 36 INPUT.

Enter market returns as the x-list:

Inputs: Item(1) = 6 INPUT; Item(2) = 10 INPUT; Item(3) = 24 INPUT; use linear model.

Output: m or slope = 1.50 = historical beta.

Graphical/numerical method: Note that this method works precisely in this problem because the data points lie in a straight line. If the plotted data points don't lie in a straight line, regression is a better method.

Slope = Rise/Run = (36 - 9)/(24 - 6) = 27/18 = 1.5. Beta = 1.5.

Step 2: *Calculate cost of equity using CAPM and beta and given inputs:*

$k_s = k_{RF} + (MRP)Beta = 7.0\% + (6.0\%)1.5 = 16.0\%$.

Financial calculator solution:

Step 3: *Calculate MIRR:*

Terminal value: using TVM
Inputs: N = 3; I = 16; PV = 0; PMT = -1,000. Output: FV = $3,505.60.

Terminal value: using cash flows
Inputs: CF_0 = 0; CF_1 = 1,000; N_j = 3; I = 16. Output: NFV = $3,505.60.

Note: Some calculators do not have Net Future Value (NFV) function. You can still calculate the NFV or terminal value using cash flows to calculate NPV, then TVM to calculate NFV or FV from the NPV.

Calculate NPV of cash inflows:

Inputs: CF_0 = 0; CF_1 = 1,000; N_j = 3; I = 16.
Output: NPV = -$2,245.89.

Now take the NPV of $2,245.89 and bring it forward at 16% for three periods to get the FV or terminal value.

Copyright © 1996 by The Dryden Press. All rights reserved.

```
Inputs:   N = 3; I = 16; PV = -2,245.89; PMT = 0.
Output:   FV = $3,505.60.

MIRR:  using TVM
Inputs:   N = 3; PV = -2,028; PMT = 0; FV = 3,505.60.
Output:   I = 20.01 = MIRR ≈ 20%.
```

CHAPTER 11

1.   **Time line:**

Determine the residual cash flows by subtracting the cash flows of Project S from Project M:

```
                 0        1        2        3        4  Years
                 |--------|--------|--------|--------|
Project M:    -700      265      265      265      265
Project S:    -200       85      140      130
Project M-S:  -500      180      125      135      265
```

Financial calculator solution:

Calculate the IRR of the residual cash flows, Project$_{M-S}$:

```
Inputs:   CF_0 = -500; CF_1 = 180; CF_2 = 125; CF_3 = 135; CF_4 = 265.
Output:   IRR = 14.19%.
```

When each of the projects is evaluated at a cost of capital of 14.19%, the NPVs are approximately equal. This is the rate at which McQueen should be indifferent between the two projects.

Check answer by evaluating each project at a rate of 14.19%:

```
Project M:
Inputs:   CF_0 = -700; CF_1 = 265; N_j = 4; I = 14.19.
Output:   NPV = $69.14.

Project S:
Inputs:   CF_0 = -200; CF_1 = 85; CF_2 = 140; CF_3 = 130; I = 14.19.
Output:   NPV = $69.11.
```

2.   **Time lines:**   (In thousands)

```
Jet A:   0   I=12%  1        2        3            7                        14 Years
         |----------|--------|--------|----●●●----|---------------------------|
CF_0 = -2,000     520      520      520          520

Jet B:   0   I=12%  1        2        3            7        8        9         14 Years
         |----------|--------|--------|----●●●----|--------|--------|---●●●----|
CF_0 = -6,200   1,012    1,012    1,012        1,012    1,012    1,012       1,012
```

Copyright © 1996 by The Dryden Press. All rights reserved.

Financial calculator solution:

Calculate NPV of single, 7-year project for Jet A:

Inputs: CF_0 = -2,000,000; CF_1 = 520,000; N_j = 7; I = 12.
Output: NPV = $373,153.40.

Calculate NPV of single, 14-year project for Jet B:

Inputs: CF_0 = -6,200,000; CF_1 = 1,012,000; N_j = 14; I = 12.
Output: NPV = $507,706.25.

Calculate the NPV of the 7-year project (Jet A), using replacement chain analysis:

Time line: (In thousands)

Inputs: CF_0 = -2,000,000; CF_1 = 520,000; N_j = 6; CF_2 = -1,480,000;
CF_3 = 520,000; N_j = 7; I = 12.
Output: NPV = $541,949.05.

By the replacement chain method, the Jet A project replicated is the higher NPV project, and will increase the value of the firm by $541,949.05.

3. *Calculate the breakpoints for retained earnings*

$$BP_{RE} = \frac{NI(1 - Payout)}{Equity\ fraction} = \frac{\$10,000,000(0.5)}{0.8} = \$6,250,000.$$

Calculate the component costs of capital

k_d = 0.08(1 - 0.34) = 0.0528 = 5.28%.

$k_s = \dfrac{\$5.00}{\$50.00} + 0.10 = 0.20 = 20.0\%.$

$k_c = \dfrac{\$5.00}{\$50.00(1 - 0.15)} + 0.10 = 0.2176 = 21.76\%.$

———————————— BLUEPRINTS: SOLUTIONS ————————————

Copyright © 1996 by The Dryden Press. All rights reserved.

Determine the weighted average cost of capital schedule using the optimal capital structure weights and component capital costs

$WACC_1 = 0.2(0.0528) + 0.8(0.20) = 0.1706 = 17.06\%.$
$WACC_2 = 0.2(0.0528) + 0.8(0.2176) = 0.1846 = 18.46\%.$

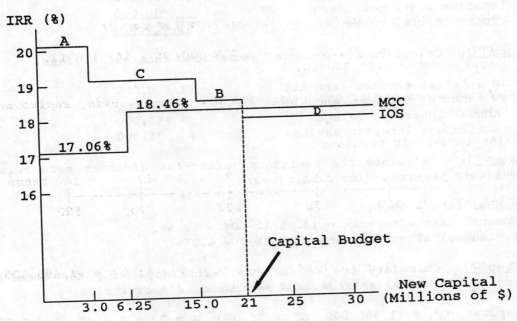

Investments A, B, and C have IRRs greater than the relevant WACC of 18.46%, therefore they should be accepted. Investment D has an IRR less than the relevant WACC and should be rejected. The optimal capital budget equals $21 million.

4. a.

5. Old bonds:

New bonds:

Copyright © 1996 by The Dryden Press. All rights reserved.

Step 1: *Calculate the number of bonds and the total initial costs of refunding (premium and flotation costs).*

Number of bonds = $10,000,000/$1,000 = 10,000 bonds.

Premium on old issue (10,000 × $100)	$1,000,000
Flotation costs new issue	400,000
Total initial costs	$1,400,000

Step 2: *Calculate the expected semiannual interest savings.*

Old interest expense (annual)	$1,500,000
New interest expense (annual)	1,350,000
Annual interest savings	$ 150,000
Semiannual interest savings	$ 75,000

Step 3: *Calculate the semiannual after-tax discount rate required to evaluate the refunding cash flows:*

Annual rate = 13.5%.
Nominal rate after-tax = 13.5%(1 − 0) = 13.5%.
Semiannual after-tax rate = 13.5%/2 = 6.75%.

Step 4: *Calculate the NPV of the refunding, using the total initial costs, semiannual savings, and semiannual discount rate:*

Inputs: $CF_0 = -1,400,000$; $CF_1 = 75,000$; $N_j = 20 \times 2 = 40$; I = 6.75.
Output: NPV = −$370,367.22 ≈ −$370,367.

This project has a negative NPV of −$370,367. Market rates would have to drop further to make the refunding a positive NPV project.

CHAPTER 12

1.　d.

2.　b.

3.　$EPS_1 = (Sales - \dfrac{Variable}{costs} - \dfrac{Fixed}{costs} - Interest)(1 - T)/Shares\ outstanding.$

Step 1 *Calculate the amount of debt and interest expense*

Debt = 0.60 × $400,000 = $240,000.
Interest = 0.12 × $240,000 = $28,800.

BLUEPRINTS: SOLUTIONS
Copyright © 1996 by The Dryden Press. All rights reserved.

Step 2 *Solve for sales using the forecasted EPS*

$$EPS_1 = \$4.00 = (S - 0.40S - \$80,000 - \$28,800) \times (1 - 0.40)/10,000$$
$$= (0.60S - \$108,800)(0.6)/10,000$$
$$\$4.00 = (0.36S - \$65,280)/10,000$$
$$\$105,280 = 0.36S$$
$$Sales = \$292,444.44 \approx \$292,445.$$

Alternative method: Note that Sales − VC − FC = EBIT. Calculate net income from EPS and shares outstanding and work back up the income statement.

$$EPS_1 = (EBIT - Interest)(1 - T)/Shares\ outstanding.$$

Solve for net income, then EBT, interest (step 1 above), and EBIT.

Net Income = EPS × Shares outstanding = \$4.00 × 10,000 = \$40,000.
EBT = NI/(1 − T) = \$40,000/(0.6) = \$66,667.
Interest (from above) = \$28,800.
EBIT = EBT + Interest = \$66,667 + \$28,800 = \$95,467.

Solve for sales using VC percentage, EBIT, and FC.

$$S = 0.40S + \$95,467 + \$80,000$$
$$0.6S = \$175,467$$
$$S = \$175,467/0.6 = \$292,445.$$

4. Degree of financial leverage:

DTL = DOL × DFL
2.0 = 1.6 × DFL
DFL = 1.25.

$$1.25 = \frac{\$4,000,000}{\$4,000,000 - I}$$

$$\$5,000,000 - 1.25(I) = \$4,000,000$$

$$I = \$800,000.$$

$$Debt = \frac{\$800,000}{0.095} = \$8,421,053.$$

Must retire = \$15,000,000 − \$8,421,053 = \$6,578,947 in bonds.

CHAPTER 13

1.   b.

Copyright © 1996 by The Dryden Press. All rights reserved.

2.   e.   The dividend irrelevance theory is MM's theory. The tax preference theory says that capital gains are preferred to dividends, while the bird-in-the-hand (G-L) theory says that dividends are preferred to capital gains. The clientele effect assumes that investors are attracted to a firm's particular dividend payout policy.

3.   *Calculate the amount of debt and interest expense (in millions)*

Total assets = $200; 40% debt × $200 = $80 million in debt.

Interest expense = $80 × 0.10 = $8.0 million.

Calculate net income (in millions)

EBIT	$98.0
less: Interest	− 8.0
EBT	$90.0
less: Taxes (@34%)	− 30.6
Net income	$59.4

Calculate portion of projects financed with retained earnings

IOS contains $60 million in positive NPV projects.
Retained earnings portion: $60M × 0.60 = $36.0 million
Debt portion: $60M × 0.40 = $24.0 million

Calculate residual available for dividends

$59.4M − $36.0M = $23.4 million in dividends.

CHAPTER 14

1.   **Formula solution:**

<u>Step 1</u>: *Use the AFN formula to calculate AFN.*

$$\text{AFN} = A^*/S(\Delta S) - L^*/S(\Delta S) - M(S_1)(1 - d)$$

$$= \frac{\$10,000}{\$10,000}(\$5,000) - \frac{\$1,500}{\$10,000}(\$5,000) - 0.11(\$15,000)(1 - 0.6)$$

$$= 1(\$5,000) - 0.15(\$5,000) - 0.11(\$15,000)(0.4)$$

$$= \$5,000 - \$750 - \$660 = \$3,590.$$

<u>Step 2</u>: *Calculate the new account levels for current assets and current liabilities.*

Current assets will increase by 50% to $7,000(1.5) = $10,500.

The AFN will be funded using short-term debt.

Copyright © 1996 by The Dryden Press. All rights reserved.

Current liabilities will increase to:

$$A/P + Accruals = \$1,500(1.5) = \$2,250$$
$$S\text{-}T\ Debt = \$2,000 + \$3,590 = 5,590$$
$$Total\ C.L. = \underline{\$7,840}$$

Calculate the new current ratio:

New current ratio = $10,500/$7,840 = 1.34.

2. Construct a partial projected income statement and balance sheet:

	Last Year	Forecast Basis	First Pass	Feedback	Second Pass
EBIT	$ 240,000	× 1.10	$ 264,000		$ 264,000
– Interest	80,000	–	80,000	+ 3,990	83,990
EBT	$ 160,000		$ 184,000		$ 180,010
– Taxes	64,000	–	73,600	–	72,004
NI	$ 96,000		$ 110,400		$ 108,006
NI avail. to common	$ 96,000		$ 110,400		$ 108,006
Divs. to common (37,800 × $1.27)	48,006	37,800 × 1.40	52,920	+ 1,023	53,943
Addition to RE	$ 47,994		$ 57,480		$ 54,063
Total assets	$1,100,000	× 1.10	$1,210,000		$1,210,000
Accruals	$ 13,636	× 1.10	$ 15,000		$ 15,000
Long-term debt	640,000		640,000	+ 30,694	670,694
Equity	335,000		335,000	+ 20,462	355,462
RE	111,364	+ 57,480	168,844	– 3,417	165,427
Total liab & equity	$1,100,000		$1,158,844		$1,206,583
AFN			51,156		3,417
Cumulative AFN			$51,156		$54,573

AFN financing (first pass)

The shortfall will be financed in accordance with the capital structure.

Long-term debt	0.60 × $51,156 =	$30,694
Common stock	0.40 × $51,156 =	20,462
		$51,156

The increase in long-term debt from the first pass is $30,694. The interest rate on the new debt is 13%. Thus, the financing feedback additional interest expense is $30,694(0.13) = $3,990.

Copyright © 1996 by The Dryden Press. All rights reserved.

Use the current stock price and required new common equity to determine how many shares will be sold and the additional dividends to be paid.

Increase in shares of common stock: $20,462/$28 = 731 shares.
Change in dividends to pay out: 731 additional shares × $1.40 = $1,023.

AFN second pass = $3,417, which is due to feedback effects from additional interest expense and dividends. The cumulative AFN = $51,156 + $3,417 = $54,573.

3.   d.

CHAPTER 15

1.   **Time line:**

Financial calculator solution:

Calculate the market value of the bonds, V_B, today, at t = 1 on the time line above, using the new market rate.

Inputs: N = 19; I = 9.5/2 = 4.75; PMT = 35,000; FV = 1,000,000.
Output: PV = −$845,807.80.

Calculate the capital loss on the bonds. They were purchased at par for $1,000,000, but are resold 6 months later for considerably less.

Capital loss on bonds = $1,000,000 − $845,807.80 = $154,192.20.

2.   d.

3.   c.

Copyright © 1996 by The Dryden Press. All rights reserved.

4. Construct simplified comparative balance sheet and income statement for the restricted and relaxed policies (in thousands):

	15% of Sales Restricted	25% of Sales Relaxed
Balance sheet accounts:		
Current assets	$ 60	$100
Fixed assets	100	100
Total assets	$160	$200
Debt	80	100
Equity	80	100
Total liabilities and equity	$160	$200
Income statement accounts:		
EBIT	36.0	36.0
Less: Interest (10%)	(8.0)	(10.0)
EBT	28.0	26.0
Less: Taxes (40%)	(11.2)	(10.4)
Net income	$16.8	$15.6

Calculate ROEs under each policy:

ROE = NI/Equity = $16.8/$80 = 0.21; $15.6/$100 = 0.156.
ROE (restricted policy) = 21.0%.
ROE (relaxed policy) = 15.6%.
Difference in ROEs = 0.21 - 0.156 = 0.054 = 5.4%.

5. Solution: (Accounts balances stated in millions)

Old	With Change

Inventory conversion period:

$$ICP = \frac{360}{\frac{40}{10}} = \frac{360}{4} = 90. \qquad \frac{360}{\frac{40}{8}} = \frac{360}{5} = 72.$$

Receivables conversion period (or days sales outstanding):

$$DSO = \frac{8}{\frac{40}{360}} = \frac{8}{\frac{1}{9}} = 72. \qquad \frac{7}{\frac{40}{360}} \quad \frac{7}{\frac{1}{9}} = 63.$$

Copyright © 1996 by The Dryden Press. All rights reserved.

Payables deferral period:

DP = 30 days - 30   DP   - 30
        CCC = $\overline{132}$ days   New CCC = $\overline{105}$ days

Change in CCC = 132 - 105 = 27 days.
Net change is -27 days (CCC is 27 days shorter).

CHAPTER 16

1.   **Financial calculator solution:**

(1)   Simple interest: 13.0%. EAR = 13.0%.

(2)   Renewable loan: The rate on this loan is essentially a 12% nominal annual rate with quarterly compounding. Calculate the EAR.

      Inputs: NOM% = 12; P/YR = 4. Output: EFF% = 12.55%.

(3)   Trade credit: Terms 1/30, net 60.

      Note that the approximate rate is really the rate per period multiplied by the number of periods, or a nominal annual rate.

      1/99 × 360/(60 - 30) = 0.0101 × 12 = 12.12% approximate rate.

      Calculate the EAR using the interest rate conversion feature:

      Inputs: NOM% = 12.12; P/YR = 12. Output: EFF% = 12.82%.

The least expensive type of credit is the quarterly renewable loan at 12.55% effective annual rate.

2.   d.

Copyright © 1996 by The Dryden Press. All rights reserved.